Harry Potter™

FEASTS
&
FESTIVITIES

FROM THE FILMS OF

Harry Potter

™

FEASTS
&
FESTIVITIES

AN OFFICIAL BOOK OF MAGICAL
CELEBRATIONS, CRAFTS, AND PARTY FOOD
INSPIRED BY THE WIZARDING WORLD

JENNIFER CARROLL

INSIGHT ◉ EDITIONS

San Rafael • Los Angeles • London

Contents

119 THE YULE BALL Holiday Celebration

INTRODUCTION

Few film worlds have captured our hearts and imaginations as completely as the magical world of the Harry Potter films. From *Harry Potter and the Sorcerer's Stone* to *Harry Potter and the Deathly Hallows – Parts 1* and *2*, each movie takes us on a journey of adventure, curiosity, inspiration, and celebration. From decadent feasts in the Great Hall to more modest holiday celebrations at Grimmauld Place, there are many memorable gatherings and events featured across the eight movies of the Harry Potter series. Now, with this official guide, you can bring a touch of Potter magic to your own celebrations. From a House Cup Birthday Bash to a Wizarding Wedding Reception, we've created a comprehensive guide to help you entertain in true wizarding style!

The first step in your journey to Potter party perfection is choosing your theme. This book includes five fantastic party themes complete with crafts, décor, menu suggestions, and free downloadable printables to help you re-create these wonderful events in your own home. While each party is specifically themed to a particular occasion like a birthday, Halloween, or wedding, feel free to mix and match elements from the various gatherings to create your own unique soiree. Craft a snowy Yule Ball backdrop (The Yule Ball Holiday Celebration, page 124). Delight your friends with a crafted felt Sorting Hat (Hogwarts House Cup Birthday Bash, page 44). Entertain guests with a game of Quidditch Bean Bag Toss (A Wizarding Wedding Reception, page 186). Original artwork from the films has been incorporated into the crafts and projects, meaning your party will have an extra authentic touch you can't find anywhere else. All of the templates are available for free at www.insighteditions.com/feastsandfestivities. Just visit the website, download, print, and you're ready to start crafting.

Each party also includes a variety of menu suggestions featuring recipes inspired by the films. From buffet-friendly savory dishes like the Defeating the Basilisk Sausage Roll to decorative desserts like the Patronus Charm Pull Cake, these recipes are easy to make and perfect for feeding a crowd—exactly what you need when planning a big event. Each recipe is designed to be flexible; dishes featuring meat can easily be altered to be vegetarian or vegan by swapping out the protein for extra veggies, and regular flour can be substituted for your preferred gluten-free mix.

As you read through the book, keep an eye out for behind-the-scenes insights, quotes, fun facts, concept art, and film stills to help further inspire your party planning and deepen your knowledge of the story. So, sit back, pour yourself a glass of Whomping Willow Punch, and prepare to explore the Wizarding World of Harry Potter one party at a time!

TIPS AND TRICKS FOR PLANNING A MAGICAL CELEBRATION

In *Harry Potter and the Deathly Hallows – Part 1*, we see the Weasleys whip out their wands and raise a party tent with ease. Unfortunately, everyday party planning isn't always so simple. The secret to success lies in the very name: planning. When creating an epic Harry Potter celebration, it's imperative to plan and prepare carefully so you are able to enjoy the festivities alongside your guests. After all, you don't want to miss any magical moments!

To help you make the most of your efforts, here are 10 steps to achieve party-planning wizardry.

1. PLAN YOUR PURPOSE

Think about why you are hosting the party. What is its purpose? Is it a just-for-fun get-together, or are you celebrating a milestone? Are there any specific goals you are hoping to achieve? Friends you want to introduce to each other? Neighbors you want to meet? Clients or coworkers you hope to impress? It's important to clarify why you're celebrating so you can help incorporate these goals into your party plan.

2. SET A BUDGET

Now that you know why you're having a party, you need to set your budget. How much do you want to spend overall? Once you have a specific number, you can break it down by category. What's your budget for food, drinks, entertainment, rentals, location (if not at your home), flowers, decorations, etc. Proper budgeting is a key element in low-stress planning, because few things cause more stress than money. Knowing how much you have to spend from the beginning will help you find ways to stick to it. It is so easy to get swept up by the party spirit and begin overspending in the heat of the moment when you see all the beautiful possibilities. Your budget will help you stay focused and not get into hot water.

Much of your spending will likely go to food and drinks. While there are no hard and fast rules for how to precisely budget for this, here are a couple of general tips to guide you.

FOOD

- When serving hors d'oeuvres, allow four to six servings per guest before a meal, or allow this same amount per hour if there is no meal.
- If serving a meal, either buffet or seated, allow approximately 6 ounces of meat/fish/poultry per person, 1½ ounces of grains, 5 ounces of potatoes, and 4 ounces of vegetables per person. Having bread, nuts, and other finger snacks on hand can help fill up any extra-hungry guests.
- Finally, allow two to three small servings of dessert for guests if you are serving multiple options or one full-size serving if you're limiting your selection to one sweet.

DRINKS

- In general, estimate two drinks per guest per hour for the first hour, then one drink per hour for every additional hour.
- If serving dessert, don't forget to offer coffee or tea as well.

ABOVE: The Halloween feast in the Great Hall, from *Harry Potter and the Sorcerer's Stone.*

3. MAKE A LIST

There's an old saying, "If you fail to plan, you plan to fail." This is true for so many parts of our lives, and entertaining is certainly one. Don't be like Harry the night before the second task, with no idea what's going to happen the next day. Make a plan. Better yet, make a list. We have provided a handy party-planning checklist you can download to help get you started. Once you have your list made, don't forget to keep checking it. Follow-through is key to staying on track.

4. PICK A THEME & MEMORABLE-MOMENT ACTIVITIES

Once you know your "why," make it more personal and exciting for you and your guests by pairing it with a theme. In the coming chapters, we provide you with multiple themes, several of which can be modified to suit your purpose. For example, the House Points Birthday Party could just as easily be applied to a graduation celebration.

After choosing your theme, pick at least one fun and fabulous element to make your party stand out and live long in the memories of your guests. In these next pages we give you perfectly paired suggestions for each party to help you on your way to (event) greatness!

5. INVITE YOUR GUESTS

While the Harry Potter films might make us long for the flourish of owl post, most people must rely on more traditional methods of inviting our guests. Thanks to the magic of technology, you may now invite friends via email, but take note, nothing sparks a guest's imagination and excitement quite like a creative invitation they can hold in their hand. We've designed six beautiful party invitations for this book to help you generate anticipation for your special event.

INVITATION BASICS

- Send out your invitations three to four weeks prior to the party.
- Be sure to include any special directions on your invitation. Should guests dress in costume? May they bring a guest? Should they bring a gift? These are common questions you may need to address.
- Include RSVP details and a date by when they should respond. This will help you manage your planning and preparation.
- Keep a few extra invites on hand for last-minute changes.
- Proofread your invitations before sending them. Double-check the date, time, location, etc.
- If your party is formal, make sure to note the dress code.
- For casual parties, feel free to send an email invitation, but if the party is meant to be more formal, it is traditional to send a printed version.

6. AUTOMATE

Wherever possible, incorporate self-serve options to keep your running-around time to a minimum. Of course, it's great to hire staff for a big party, but even a couple of teenage helpers can make a big impact on an at-home gathering. Easy ways to automate include food-and-drink stations and activities like a photo booth or other icebreaker craft that can be set up in advance and don't require you to operate them.

ABOVE: Luna and Harry en route to Professor Slughorn's Christmas Party. NEXT PAGE: Slughorn's office was lavishly decorated for his Christmas Party in *Harry Potter and the Half-Blood Prince*.

7. CREATE ZONES

If you are hosting a mix of kids and grown-ups, create designated spaces for each where they can feel comfortable. They can be in the same room—think kids' table and grown-ups' table. The point is to offer areas that will engage and interest all of your guests. You can even name them to match your theme (i.e. "All Kids to the Gryffindor Common Room, Adults to the Great Hall"). Happy kids equal happy parents, which always means a better party! Create drop zones for trash and dirty dishes (subdivide into categories like flatware, glasses, and plates for easier cleanup and recycling later).

8. ASSIGN DUTIES

Especially when entertaining at home, it is so easy for one person to get stuck with all the cleanup at the end of a party. The old saying "many hands make light work" is never truer than at the end of a wonderful evening when you are tired and ready to rest but looking at a space that's messier than a student common room after a Quidditch match! Discuss end-of-party roles with all hosts or family members to minimize misunderstandings and help cleanup be a breeze.

9. SET UP AHEAD

Do everything you can ahead of time. Prepare as much food in advance as possible, set the tables the night before, etc. To save time during cooking, feel free to use store-bought options for certain ingredients, such as pizza sauce or pepper jelly. On party day, you want to be fresh, not exhausted before the festivities even begin. Purposefully give yourself about an hour before guests are due to arrive to have a moment to catch your breath, calm down, and prepare to enjoy your hard work!

10. BON VOYAGE

The hallmark of a good party is good food and good company. Once you've covered the menu, it's always a good idea to make a little extra effort to send guests home with something special as a token of appreciation for their presence. Plan a sweet send-off by packing up a delectable treat or gift for them to take away as a thank-you. They will remember your thoughtfulness, and it will leave a sweet taste in their mouth and memory.

Hogwarts House Cup Birthday Bash

"Welcome, welcome to another year at Hogwarts!"

Professor Dumbledore, *Harry Potter and the Prisoner of Azkaban*

HOGWARTS HOUSE CUP BIRTHDAY BASH

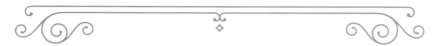

In the Harry Potter films, new students at Hogwarts are sorted into four houses upon arrival at the Great Hall. Each house's students are renowned for specific character traits. Gryffindors often demonstrate bravery and chivalry, Hufflepuffs tend to be loyal, patient, and hard-working, Ravenclaws excel at wit and learning, and Slytherins value cunning and ambition. Once sorted into their houses by the Sorting Hat, students are extremely loyal to them and work throughout the year to earn points to win the coveted house cup.

Inspired by the four houses, this colorful birthday party is your opportunity to show your house pride. Ideal for all ages, this event allows quite a bit of personalization—you can customize the party to your particular house or create an all-inclusive bash featuring all four. The party includes a treasure chest of DIY decorations and favors in the house colors: House Flag Pennants, House Crest Pins, even a festive birthday banner reading "Happee Birthdae"—in honor of Harry's first birthday cake, of course. The menu suggestions are also largely house-themed, with dishes perfect for feeding a crowd like the Hogwarts House Party Pizzas and fun dessert options like the Sorting Ceremony Ice Cream Sundaes (with a colorful surprise inside!).

Fans who already know their houses can come dressed in their preferred house colors, while the host can hold a Sorting Ceremony for those guests who have yet to be assigned to a house with our DIY Sorting Hat—which can actually "talk"! Not sure of your own house? Find out through the official Sorting Experience, created by J.K. Rowling herself, at https://www.wizardingworld.com/news/discover-your-hogwarts-house-on-wizarding-world.

Are you ready to represent your house? Let the Sorting begin!

EVENT OVERVIEW

INVITATION
- Hogwarts House Cup Birthday Bash Invites

DECORATIONS
- "Happee Birthdae" Banner in House Colors
- Handheld House Flag Pennants
- House Serving Boards
- Floating Candles
- House Points Display

MENU SUGGESTIONS
- Moony's Transformational Cheesy Pasta Balls
- Luna Lovegood's Rainbow Radish Slaw
- Hogwarts House Party Pizzas
- Hagrid's "Happee Birthdae" Cupcakes
- Sorting Ceremony Ice Cream Sundaes
- Whomping Willow Punch

ACTIVITIES
- Sorting Hat & Ceremony
- House Points Charades Competition

FAVORS
- House Traits Bookmarks

HOGWARTS HOUSE CUP BIRTHDAY BASH INVITES

Little more than a swish of your mouse and a tap of your keyboard is needed to invite your fellow witches and wizards to this celebration, thanks to our printable invitation template. There are five options, one general Hogwarts-themed design, as well as one for each house, giving you the option to fully customize your party.

- Hogwarts House Cup Birthday Party Invitation template ⊙
- White cardstock
- A7 envelopes, in your color of choice

1. Download the Hogwarts House Cup Birthday Party Invitation template from our online resources. Select the invitation design to suit your party theme.

2. Open the invitation in Adobe Reader. Fill in the details for your party in the editable fields.

3. Print the invitations on white cardstock. Put each invitation in an envelope and seal.

4. Stamp your envelopes, address them, and put them the post! Alternatively, you can send the PDF invitations as an email attachment if you distrust any post not sent by owl.

RIGHT: Gryffindor students celebrate their victory on the Quidditch pitch—and Ron's success as Keeper—in *Harry Potter and the Half-Blood Prince*.

LET'S CELEBRATE

YOU'RE INVITED TO A GRYFFINDOR HOUSE
BIRTHDAY PARTY IN HONOUR OF

Harry Potter

Grab your floo powder, a portkey, or board the
Hogwarts's Express and meet us

July 31

4:00 PM
Potter Residence
12 Grimmauld Place

OWL POST REPLY

7.13 to Ginny Potter – 310.123.9876

Please come dressed in your house colors.
Don't have a house yet? You'll be sorted upon arrival.

LET'S CELEBRATE

YOU'RE INVITED TO A HOGWARTS ALL-HOUSE
BIRTHDAY PARTY IN HONOUR OF

Percy Weasley

Grab your floo powder, a portkey, or board the
Hogwarts's Express and meet us

August 22

4:00 PM
The Burrow
1 Ottery Way

OWL POST REPLY

8.10 to Mrs. Weasley – 310.123.9876

Please come dressed in your house colors.
Don't have a house yet? You'll be sorted upon arrival.

"HAPPEE BIRTHDAE" BANNER
IN HOUSE COLORS

Add festive house colors to your decor while celebrating the birthday witch or wizard with this easy banner reading "Happee Birthdae"—just the way Hagrid writes it when he presents Harry with his very first birthday cake.

- "Happee Birthdae" Banner printable ⬇
- White cardstock
- Scissors
- Hole punch
- Ribbon or string
- Tape or Command strip hooks

1. Download the "Happee Birthdae" Banner from our online resources.

2. Print each banner flag on white cardstock, and cut them out individually.

3. Punch two holes along the base of each triangle (the triangles point downward). We recommend one in each corner.

4. Feed the ribbon or string through punched holes to link the flags together and create your banner.

5. Attach to your wall with tape, Command strip hooks, or other adhesive.

Styling Magic!

The Gryffindor common room was designed for a "reassuring feeling of warmth and comfort, with a beat-up sofa, a threadbare carpet, and a massive fireplace." The last was incredibly important to Stuart Craig, as the common room is the first warm, comforting home experience Harry has ever had. So the hearth became the center of the room draped in lush tapestries and rich red carpets.

When styling your space for the Hogwarts House Cup Bash, take a leaf out of Craig's book, and go for a warm, welcoming, and colorful vibe. This party can be themed to one house or all four, and the décor should reflect that in your choice of linens and tableware. The Floating Candles can go over the buffet table or the welcome area where the Sorting takes place. Extra touches like balloons, streamers, and Hogwarts house banners will add an additional dose of festivity and Harry Potter magic!

ABOVE: A set photo of the Gryffindor common room.

HANDHELD HOUSE FLAG PENNANTS

These pennants add color and house pride to your party décor. Simply download the designs from our online resources section and print them. The pennants can be attached directly to the wall, hung with ribbon like a garland, or attached to wooden dowels and placed throughout your party space wherever you need a pop of color.

- House Flag Pennant printables ⊙
- White cardstock
- Scissors
- Ribbon, string, or dowels
- Double-sided tape or your preference for displaying

1. Download the House Flag Pennant printables from our online resources.

2. Print each pennant on white cardstock, and cut them out individually.

3. Fold tabs around ribbon or dowels if using, and secure with double-sided tape. Otherwise, attach to wall or other surface with tape as desired.

HOUSE SERVING BOARDS

Elevate your party buffet with these House Serving Boards. The wooden boards, which sport the mascots for each house, are ideal serving platters for many items on your menu including the Hogwarts House Party Pizzas and Hagrid's "Happee Birthdae" Cupcakes. These would also make fun prizes to award lucky guests.

- House Serving Board pattern ⬇
- Adhesive vinyl or heat transfer vinyl (HTV) in your preferred house colors
- Transfer paper
- Electric cutting machine (Cricut) or scissors
- Wooden serving boards
- Heat press, if using HTV (optional)

1. Download the pattern for the House Serving Boards from our online resources. If you are using a cutting machine such as a Cricut, upload the SVG version of the design to your design software, and cut according to machine and material directions. If you are hand-cutting the design, print the PDF version and cut it out, then use the cutout as your template to cut the final design out of vinyl.

2. Using a weeding tool or sharp tweezers, weed the excess vinyl from your design, and place transfer paper over the image. Use your hand or a credit card to firmly press the transfer paper to your design to ensure it sticks, then gently peel the paper away from the original vinyl backing so the image of the house animal adheres to the transfer paper. Apply the cut vinyl design to your wooden cutting board, then remove the transfer paper.

TIP
Heat transfer vinyl can often create a stronger bond to wood, so consider using HTV and a heat source (such as an iron or a Cricut EasyPress) to help increase the longevity and durability of your craft.

FLOATING CANDLES

The Great Hall's iconic floating candles are one of the first things Harry (and film viewers) notice when the amazing set first appears onscreen in Harry Potter and the Sorcerer's Stone. *So of course it is a craft we had to share with you. This simple replica of the famous set prop is one you will be able to re-create again and again to build your own buoyant collection. Remote-controlled tea lights complete the effect to make your Great Hall feel truly magical.*

- 8½-by-11-inch white cardstock
- Remote-controlled tea lights
- White hot glue
- Glue gun
- Pin
- Fishing line
- Scissors

1. Roll your cardstock into a tube to loosen up the paper.

2. Roll the cardstock around the base of your remote-controlled tea light, creating a taper with the light sitting at the top. Hot-glue the cardstock together so it holds its taper shape. Once your taper is secure, slide the tea light out to complete the next steps.

3. Use a pin to poke a hole all the way through the top of your tube.

4. String fishing line through the holes. (Use different lengths of line for each candle so your candles "float" at different levels.)

5. Use hot glue to create wax drips all around the tube. Make sure you include wax drips along the seam of where you glued the cylinder together to disguise it.

6. Trace your tea light on a piece of white cardstock, and then cut out the circle. Hot glue it to the bottom of your candle and use more hot glue to create wax drips to cover up any seams.

7. Add your tea light to the top, resting it on the fishing line at the top of your taper.

8. Repeat this for as many candles as you want.

9. Hang your lights from the ceiling, and use the remote to turn them on and off.

Behind the Magic

The floating candles in the Great Hall were originally created as a practical effect, using 370 real candles suspended by wires 10 to 15 feet above the actors' heads. While the effect was breathtaking, the candles faced numerous practical challenges: The wind would blow them out, or the flames would cause the wires to break and the candles to fall. In the end, for both practical and safety reasons, the candles were redone as a special effect.

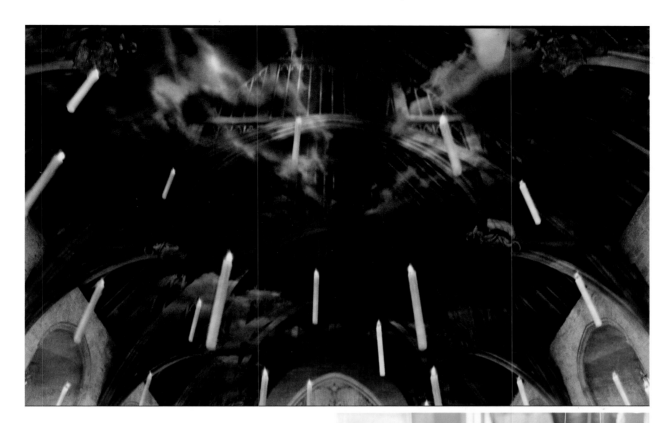

"IT'S BEWITCHED TO LOOK LIKE
THE SKY OUTSIDE. I READ ABOUT
IT IN *HOGWARTS: A HISTORY*."

Hermione Granger,
Harry Potter and the Sorcerer's Stone

ABOVE: The ceiling of the Great Hall is bewitched to look like
the sky outside.

HOUSE POINTS DISPLAY

Once your guests are Sorted, their actions both positive and negative can win or lose them those highly desired house points—which you, as the host, control. To help you and your guests keep track of their progress, make your own simple display, inspired by the enormous eye-catching prop that hangs on the wall of the Great Hall.

- 4 tall, skinny jars with screw-on lids
- Taper candlestick holders
- Gold spray paint
- House Crest templates ⬇
- Electric cutting machine (Cricut)
- Vinyl in red, yellow, green, and blue

- Vinyl transfer tape
- Scraper or credit card
- Hot glue and glue gun
- Water beads in red, yellow, green, and blue
- Water

Behind the Magic

The House Points Hourglasses featured in the Great Hall in the films are meant to appear to be filled with precious gems (emeralds, yellow diamonds, rubies, and sapphires). Instead of jewels, production designer Stuart Craig loaded the hourglasses with tens of thousands of glass beads, which caused a national shortage in England.

1. Remove the lids from the jars. Working outside, spray-paint both the jar lids and the candlestick holders gold. Allow a few hours to dry.

2. Download the House Crest templates from our online resources. Use a cutting machine to cut the house crests from vinyl in corresponding colors: Gryffindor in red, Slytherin in green, Hufflepuff in yellow, and Ravenclaw in blue.

3. Use transfer tape to transfer a house crest to each of the jars. To do this, cover each of your designs with the tape, and peel it off the vinyl backing. If your design isn't sticking to the tape, try using a scraper to help it adhere to the tape. Place the tape over your jar, vinyl side down, and smooth out the design. Use the scraper to press the design against the jar. Peel the tape slowly off the jar, leaving the design behind.

4. Hot-glue the bottom of each jar to a candlestick holder.

5. Fill the bottom of each jar with a small amount of water beads to start out.

6. At the beginning of your party, fill the jars about two-thirds full with water. Screw on the lids so no one can steal points!

7. Add more beads to the jars throughout the party to track each house's points.

8. Check at the end of the party to see whose jars are the most full and who wins the house cup.

TIP

The house cup can be anything you like. A special favor? An actual trophy? Simple bragging rights? You decide!

Moony's Transformational Cheesy Pasta Balls

Shaped like miniature full moons, these breaded pasta balls are "transformed" into crispy, delicious deep-fried goodness with a just a few minutes in the deep frier. Easy to make and even easier to eat, they make the perfect party appetizer for guests to graze on throughout the evening.

Yield: approximately 24 balls

FOR THE PASTA

6 tablespoons (¾ stick) unsalted butter
⅓ cup all-purpose flour
2 cups milk
1 cup heavy cream
1 teaspoon hot sauce
3 cups shredded sharp cheddar cheese
2 cups shredded Italian-blend cheese
1 pound elbow macaroni or pasta of choice, cooked
Salt and fresh ground black pepper

FOR THE BALLS

3 cups prepared macaroni and cheese, chilled
2 cups frying oil such as canola or safflower
2 eggs, beaten
1½ cups panko bread crumbs
Ranch dressing or marinara sauce, for dipping if desired

SPECIAL SUPPLIES

1-inch cookie scoop

TO MAKE THE PASTA

In a large saucepan over medium heat, melt butter. Add the flour, and cook over medium heat for approximately 3 minutes, stirring constantly with a wooden spoon. Be careful to not let the flour brown.

Add the milk and heavy cream, whisking constantly to avoid forming lumps, until mixture is smooth and slightly thickened.

Stir in hot sauce and cheeses, and continue stirring until cheese has melted. Add salt and pepper to taste.

Add cooked pasta, and stir to coat all noodles.

Pour prepared pasta into a covered baking pan, and allow to cool for at least 4 hours or overnight.

TO MAKE THE BALLS

Line a baking sheet with parchment paper.

Once pasta has cooled, use a 1-inch cookie scoop to form 1-inch balls of pasta.

Place balls on lined baking sheet, and set tray in freezer for 15 minutes to set.

Meanwhile, add the oil to a heavy cooking pot such as a Dutch oven or large high-side skillet fitted with a frying thermometer, and heat to 350°F.

Set up your dredging stations. Add the beaten eggs to a small bowl, and pour the bread crumbs out onto a high-sided plate or baking dish. Dip frozen macaroni and cheese balls in eggs, then roll firmly in breadcrumbs to help them adhere. Working in small batches, carefully place balls in hot oil to fry for 3 to 4 minutes or until golden brown. Remove with a metal slotted spoon.

Drain on paper towels, and serve immediately. These can be served plain or with your favorite dipping sauce, such as ranch or marinara.

LUNA LOVEGOOD'S RAINBOW RADISH SLAW

While it could be argued that many wizarding families have their quirks, the Lovegood family— kind, dreamy Ravenclaw Luna and her editor father—cheerfully push the limit on eccentricity with everything from their self-published newspaper The Quibbler *to their eye-catching wardrobe choices. One of Luna's signature accessories is her dirigible plum earrings, which were designed and crafted by actress Evanna Lynch herself. Dirigible plums are a unique wizarding fruit that look similar to radishes, but grow upside down. This bright and colorful radish slaw, inspired by Luna's iconic earrings, is the perfect side dish for a barbecue, garden party, or any event that calls for food that stands out as much as the Lovegoods do.*

YIELD: 8 TO 10 SERVINGS

FOR THE DRESSING
½ cup light olive oil
¼ cup apple cider vinegar
2 tablespoons Dijon mustard
3 tablespoons honey
½ teaspoon salt
¼ teaspoon sumac

FOR THE SLAW
1 small head napa cabbage, sliced into thin ribbons
1 small head radicchio, sliced into thin ribbons
4 to 5 Easter Egg radishes, scrubbed and stemmed
2 yellow carrots, scrubbed and stemmed
3 purple, red, or orange carrots, scrubbed and stemmed

TO MAKE THE DRESSING

In a small bowl, whisk all the dressing ingredients, and set aside.

TO MAKE THE SLAW

With a sharp knife, slice radishes and yellow carrots into thin rounds. Shred the other carrots on the large side of a box grater.

Mix all the slaw ingredients in a large bowl, add the dressing, and toss.

Slaw can be served right away or refrigerated overnight.

TIP
Include a clever nod to another famous Luna accessory—the Spectrespecs—by styling this dish with two large slices of radish in the center of your slaw.

Hogwarts House Party Pizzas

What's the one thing any student gathering needs? Pizza! These delicious Hogwarts House Party Pizzas are perfect for feeding a common room full of hungry guests. Shaped like a crest, there's one for every house—in their colors no less. We've got pepperoni and bell pepper for Gryffindor, spinach and pesto for Slytherin, curried turkey for Hufflepuff, and a sweet blueberry dessert pizza for Ravenclaw.

YIELD: 6 SAVORY PIZZAS AND
8 DESSERT PIZZAS

FOR THE SAVORY PIZZAS (GRYFFINDOR, SLYTHERIN, HUFFLEPUFF)

Three 1-pound packages pizza dough

One 16-ounce jar of your favorite pizza sauce

One 12-ounce jar of your favorite pesto sauce

1 pound shredded mozzarella cheese

SLYTHERIN TOPPINGS

4 cups roughly chopped baby spinach

1 tablespoon olive oil

1 tablespoon balsamic vinegar

½ pound mushrooms, diced

One 6-ounce jar artichoke hearts, sliced thin

HUFFLEPUFF TOPPINGS

1 pound ground turkey

2 tablespoons coconut oil

2 teaspoons curry powder

½ teaspoon salt

1 teaspoon turmeric

6 ounces pitted kalamata olives

1 pint yellow cherry tomatoes

GRYFFINDOR TOPPINGS

2 red bell peppers, diced

2 yellow bell peppers, diced

8 ounces pepperoni slices

FOR THE DESSERT PIZZA (RAVENCLAW)

1 package puff pastry, defrosted according to package instructions

1 egg, lightly beaten with 1 tablespoon water, for egg wash

1 cup heavy cream plus 2 tablespoons, divided

1 teaspoon sugar

1 teaspoon vanilla extract

6 ounces dark chocolate

Two 6-ounce containers blueberries

One 6-ounce container blackberries

TO MAKE THE SAVORY PIZZAS (GRYFFINDOR, SLYTHERIN, HUFFLEPUFF)

Prepare the spinach (Slytherin):

Toss the spinach in olive oil and vinegar. Set aside.

Prepare the curried turkey (Hufflepuff):

In a medium skillet over medium-high heat, melt the coconut oil and add in the salt and spices. Stir to combine. Add in the ground turkey, and stir to break up and brown. Continue to stir until well combined with the spice mixture and cooked through, about 10 minutes. Set aside.

ASSEMBLE YOUR PIZZAS

Place two baking sheets in the oven, and preheat the oven and the sheets to 475°F.

Split each ball of pizza dough in half, and stretch into crest shapes about 6 by 12 inches.

For Hufflepuff and Gryffindor, cover four crests with tomato sauce and mozzarella cheese (make sure to save some cheese for Slytherin!). Add the toppings for Hufflepuff to two of the crests in quadrants, making stripes, squares, and other patterns with your house toppings. Repeat this process with the Gryffindor toppings on the other two crests.

For Slytherin, cover the remaining two crests with pesto sauce, mozzarella cheese, and spinach. Add the remaining toppings as you did for the other pizzas.

Transfer the pizzas to the oven, and bake 12 to 15 minutes until the crusts are golden brown and the cheese is melted and bubbling.

TO MAKE THE DESSERT PIZZA (RAVENCLAW)

Roll out each piece of puff pastry to a 10-by-15-inch rectangle. Cut each piece into fourths.

With one short end facing you, trim the opposite end to a rounded point, creating the crest shape. Save all the scraps.

When all the crests have been cut, gather the scraps, and roll them out. Cut thin strips, about a quarter-inch wide.

Use a fork to crimp the edges of all the crests, and brush with egg wash.

Use the strips to build a "wall" along the edges, from the point up both sides to the top. Leave about half an inch clear at the top.

Fold down the top to seal the strips and close the wall.

Use a fork to prick holes all over the inside of each crest.

Bake for 15 to 20 minutes or until golden brown. Check after 10 minutes and reprick the centers if they are puffing up. When the pastry is golden brown, remove from the oven, and set aside to cool while you prepare the fillings.

In a medium mixing bowl, whip 1 cup of the cream together with the sugar and vanilla until stiff peaks form.

Put the chocolate and the remaining 2 tablespoons of cream into a microwave-safe bowl. Microwave for 30 seconds, and stir to combine. If needed, continue to microwave in 10-second intervals, stirring after each time until the chocolate is completely melted.

To assemble, spread whipped cream over each crest. Create 2 diagonal quadrants with the blueberries and spoon the ganache over the 2 remaining quadrants. Decorate with a few blackberries.

HAGRID'S "HAPPEE BIRTHDAE" CUPCAKES

In Harry Potter and the Sorcerer's Stone, Harry gets his first-ever birthday cake, kindly baked by Hagrid and simply decorated with the message "HAPPEE BIRTHDAE." Inspired by that touching moment, this chocolate cupcake version of Hagrid's cake uses one letter per cupcake (extras can embellished with lightning bolts or other Potter symbolism) so your dessert table can send a warm message in a "big" way!

Yield: 24 cupcakes

FOR THE CUPCAKES

1½ cups cake flour

1 cup unsweetened cocoa powder

1 teaspoon baking powder

1 teaspoon baking soda

½ teaspoon salt

½ cup milk, at room temperature

½ cup sour cream

4 large eggs, at room temperature

1 cup granulated sugar

1 cup packed light brown sugar

½ cup plus 1 tablespoon vegetable or canola oil (or melted coconut oil)

3 teaspoons vanilla extract

FOR THE FROSTING

1 cup (2 sticks) butter, softened

8 cups powdered sugar

½ cup half-and-half

3 teaspoons vanilla extract

Pinch of salt

3 to 4 drops pink food coloring (add more or less to achieve desired color)

2 drops green food coloring (add more or less to achieve desired color)

SPECIAL SUPPLIES

Muffin pan
Cupcake liners

TO MAKE THE CUPCAKES

Preheat the oven to 350°F. Place cupcake liners in muffin pan and set aside.

In a large bowl, whisk together the flour, cocoa powder, baking powder, baking soda, and salt until combined. Set aside.

Combine milk and sour cream in a small measuring bowl or jar and set aside.

In a separate medium bowl, whisk the eggs, granulated sugar, brown sugar, oil, and vanilla until combined. Pour approximately half the egg mixture into the dry ingredients. Add half the milk and sour cream mixture, and gently whisk to begin to combine. Be careful not to overmix. Add the remaining egg mixture and milk mixture, and finish combining all ingredients until a thin batter forms.

Pour batter into prepared cupcake liners, filling each one halfway.

Bake for 18 to 20 minutes or until a toothpick comes out clean. Remove cupcakes to a wire rack, and allow to cool completely before frosting.

Repeat this until all the batter is gone. You should have at least 24 cupcakes.

Continued on page 39

TO MAKE THE FROSTING

While cakes are cooling, use a hand mixer on medium speed to cream the butter, powdered sugar, half-and-half, vanilla, and salt in a mixing bowl, scraping down sides as necessary, until light and fluffy.

Remove 1 cup of frosting to a small, separate bowl.

Add drops of pink food coloring to your main frosting bowl and continue mixing until you've achieved your desired color. Depending on the temperature in your kitchen this may take a few minutes, so stick with it.

Mix the 1 cup of reserved white icing with the green food coloring, and place in a piping bag. Set aside.

Once icing is nice and fluffy, ice the cooled cupcakes with the pink frosting. It's okay if it's a little sloppy—this is Hagrid's work you're replicating!

Once all cupcakes are frosted, pipe the letters in green icing onto the top of your cupcakes. Do one letter per cupcake to spell the message "Happee Birthdae" and decorate the rest with lightning bolts or other Harry Potter symbols.

"IT'S NOT EVERY DAY YOUR YOUNG MAN TURNS ELEVEN, NOW, IS IT?"

Rubeus Hagrid, *Harry Potter and the Sorcerer's Stone*

The Sorting Ceremony plays a key role in welcoming first-year students to Hogwarts. Now you can create your own special version with these "surprise" Sorting Hat ice cream sundaes. The secret is to fill the chocolate "hats" with colored sprinkles, which represent the corresponding houses. Your guests, both young and old, will enjoy cracking into their hats to discover their houses.

YIELD: 6 SUNDAES

6 ice cream cones

1 large chewy chocolate roll or 6 individual size rolls

10 ounces milk chocolate

House color sprinkles, about 2 teaspoons per hat

Ice cream, flavor of choice

Hot fudge sauce (optional)

SPECIAL SUPPLIES

Offset spatula

Using a sharp knife, cut the tip off each cone about 1 inch down from the point. Place the cones and their tips on a cookie sheet with a wire rack over it, and have it standing by.

Cut the chocolate roll into 1-inch pieces, and place them on a microwave-safe plate. Microwave them for 10 to 20 seconds until just softened. Do not overheat.

Use the pliable chocolate candy to "glue" the tips on the cones at an angle, making the point of the hat. Use the remaining candy to sculpt the Sorting Hat's features, eyebrows, and mouth, on the plate. Gently press the pieces onto the cones.

Melt half the chocolate in the microwave or over a double boiler, being careful not to overheat.

Use an offset spatula to spread chocolate onto each cone, contouring around the feature of the face. Wrinkles and flaw are good! Allow the cone to set up for 15 to 20 minutes, placing in the refrigerator if necessary.

Draw six 3-inch circles onto a piece of parchment. Flip the parchment over and place on a cookie sheet. Melt the remaining chocolate. Use the offset spatula to fill in the circles with a layer of chocolate about an eighth of an inch thick. Too thin and it won't hold up; too thick and it will be hard to crack. Allow to set completely, 15 to 20 minutes.

When all the chocolate hats and disks have set, assemble the cones. Remelt the leftover chocolate. Spoon about 2 teaspoons of sprinkles into a cone, smear a small amount of chocolate around the rim, and top with a chocolate disk. Place brim-down on a cookie sheet to set, and repeat with the remaining cones.

To assemble the sundae, place a large scoop of ice cream in a bowl, cover with a "strip" of hot fudge to create the side flaps of the hat. Place a cone on top. Guests can break the disk with a tap of a spoon and let the sprinkles rain down on the ice, revealing their house!

Continued on page 42

WHOMPING WILLOW PUNCH

As we see in Harry Potter and the Chamber of Secrets *and* Harry Potter and the Prisoner of Azkaban, *the Whomping Willow is not a tree to be taken lightly. It packs a punch! Inspired by this pugnacious tree, this mocktail has a real kick thanks to the tart cherry juice. Serve on its own or as a mixer.*

YIELD: 8 SERVINGS

1 cup sugar, or to taste

1 cup hot water

2½ cups lime juice

2½ cups tart cherry juice

2 tablespoons grated fresh ginger

2 cups ginger ale

Combine sugar and hot water in a small saucepan over medium heat. Bring to a simmer, stirring until sugar is completely dissolved. Remove the pan from the heat and allow the mix to cool.

In a pitcher, combine sugar syrup with lime juice, cherry juice, and fresh ginger. Stir to combine.

Slowly pour in ginger ale. Serve immediately.

HERMIONE GRANGER: "HARRY, YOU DO KNOW WHAT TREE THIS IS?"

HARRY POTTER: "THAT'S NOT GOOD. RON, RUN!"

Harry Potter and the Prisoner of Azkaban

ABOVE: The Whomping Willow sits on the Hogwarts grounds guarding a secret passage to the Shrieking Shack in *Harry Potter and the Prisoner of Azkaban.*

SORTING HAT & CEREMONY

Sorting is a critical first step for students upon arrival at Hogwarts. So too should it be for your guests. If they arrive and have yet to be assigned a house, our DIY Sorting Hat will quickly assign them. This is an easy no-sew project. For an extra magical touch, read our tip for having the Sorting Hat talk!

- 1 yard brown felt
- Pencil
- Measuring tape
- Scissors
- Tacky glue
- Needle
- Brown thread
- Mod Podge, matte finish, or craft glue substitute (see tip)
- 1-inch paintbrush or foam brush

1. Lay out your felt, and fold in half to make two layers. Make the brim of the hat by tracing one large circle about 17 inches in diameter. (Tip: Use a round pizza pan or serving platter to trace the circle.) Cut out the circle. You should have two large circles since the felt was folded.

2. Trace a smaller, 6-inch diameter circle in the center of the larger circles. Snip a little hole in the center, and then cut around your traced line.

3. Adhere the two circles together with tacky glue by applying a thick line of glue between the two circles, particularly on the outer edge.

4. With the remaining felt, trace a large triangle approximately 30 inches high with a slightly rounded bottom about 20 inches wide. This will form the cone of the hat. Cut out.

5. For the phone pocket, cut out a small rectangle of felt about an inch wider and longer than your phone (about 4 by 6 inches will fit most phones). Using a thin line of tacky glue along the bottom and side edges, attach the pocket about 3 inches from the edge of the triangle (it doesn't matter which side) and 1½ inches from the bottom.

6. Fold the two sides of the triangle together with the pocket on the inside to form the felt into the shape of a cone. Use tacky glue to seal the seam. Allow to dry for a few hours.

7. Attach the cone to the brim with tacky glue by applying a thick line around the inner circle of the brim. Press the base of the cone onto the glue. If the cone or hole is too big or small, adjust as necessary before you allow the glue to dry. At this point, it should resemble a witch's hat.

8. To make the Sorting Hat's eye sockets: On the inside of the hat, pinch the cone about 7 to 8 inches above the brim. Using a needle and thread, make a stitch, and then go over the same spot several times until it holds. Tie a knot.

9. Check the outside of the hat to make sure the eyes look the way you want them to. Adjust if necessary.

10. Crumple up paper or newsprint and place inside the cone. Paint the entire hat with crafting glue. This will make the felt heavier,

which makes the crumpled paper inside very helpful. Once it's all covered, shape your Sorting Hat by crumpling and curving the cone around the newspaper. Allow to dry for 12 to 14 hours. Once dry, remove the paper inside the cone so you can place the hat on guests' heads to Sort them into houses.

11. To make the hat "talk," place a cell phone in the pocket in the cone of the hat. Turn on the phone's speaker and have a person in another room call the phone beforehand and be ready to Sort the partygoers.

Want more inspiration for holding your own Sorting Ceremony? Visit https://www.wizarding-world.com/sorting-hat to discover your house.

HOUSE POINTS CHARADES COMPETITION

The best way for your guests to earn points for their house will be through a friendly yet challenging game of charades! Winners of each round win points while teams that don't guess correctly lose points. As the host, keep a keen eye out for good and poor sportsmanship so you can distribute extra house points as needed.

- House Points Charades Competition Cards printables ⬇
- Cardstock
- Scissors
- Bowl
- Timer

TO MAKE THE CARDS

1. Download the House Points Charades Competition Cards from the online resources, and print the pages.

2. Cut out the cards and place in a large bowl for guests to draw cards on their turn.

TO PLAY THE GAME

3. If necessary, divide guests into teams. Teams can be made up of people from the same house if the numbers are fairly evenly represented, or a mix of houses. Each individual player will be earning points for their particular house, so go with whatever is easiest for you as the host.

4. On their turn, each team will designate one player to act out the clue while the other members do their best to guess. The player acting out may not use any words— actions only!

5. Set a timer for 2 minutes for each team's turn, and have the player draw a card from the bowl. The player must play the card they draw.

6. Once the timer goes off, if the team has guessed the clue, their team is awarded points for the house(s) they represent. If they have failed to guess, they will lose house points.

7. The team with the most house points at the end of the evening wins!

TIP

Have your House Points Display handy so you can easily keep track of how each house is doing!

HOUSE TRAITS BOOKMARKS

Help your guests mark the occasion with these House Traits bookmarks, featuring some of the most significant character traits that members of each house are known to display. You can simply print and cut out the bookmarks or give them a little extra sparkle by adding some glitter and sliding them into plastic sleeves.

- House Traits Bookmarks printable
- Cardstock
- Scissors
- Glitter (in house colors)
- 2¼-by-6¼-inch plastic bookmark sleeves
- Needle and thread or heat tool (optional)

1. Download our House Traits Bookmark printable from the online resources, and print the page. Cut out the bookmarks.

2. Add a little glitter to the inside of a plastic sleeve and slide in the bookmark.

3. If you are spare with the glitter, you don't need to seal the bookmark. If you choose to add more, you may want to seal the end of the bookmark by sewing it closed or using a heat tool.

"YOUR TRIUMPHS WILL EARN YOU POINTS. ANY RULE BREAKING, AND YOU WILL LOSE POINTS. AT THE END OF THE YEAR, THE HOUSE WITH THE MOST POINTS IS AWARDED THE HOUSE CUP."

Professor McGonagall, *Harry Potter and the Sorcerer's Stone*

A Magical Creatures Halloween Party

"THE FIRST YEARS PLEASE NOTE THAT THE DARK
FOREST IS STRICTLY FORBIDDEN TO ALL STUDENTS . . ."

Professor Dumbledore, *Harry Potter and the Prisoner of Azkaban*

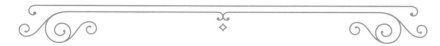

A Magical Creatures Halloween Party

Hogwarts is a wondrous place, filled with many mysterious and delightful rooms, towers, dungeons, and stairways. Yet students are warned to watch out for specific areas unless they are interested in dying a "most painful death." As the films progress, we come to learn just why these places are off-limits—particularly the Forbidden Forest. From the hungry Acromantula in *Harry Potter and the Chamber of Secrets* to the brooding centaurs in *Harry Potter and the Order of the Phoenix*, the forest is full of strange and extraordinary creatures guaranteed to make hairs stand up on your arms and chills run down your spine. Which makes it the perfect setting for a creepy, crawly Magical Creatures–themed Halloween celebration.

While this party would be ideal in an outdoor setting, it could also be easily adapted to an indoor area. Perfect for kids and adults alike, a moody, earthy color scheme helps set the tone for this spooky soiree, while a veritable menagerie of magical creatures pops up in the décor, crafts, menu, and activities to give you a friendly fright throughout the night. Easy DIY decorations including a Forbidden Forest Balloon Backdrop (complete with giant spider legs), a directional sign featuring your favorite Harry Potter destinations, and larger-than-life Nagini made out of pumpkins are added to more traditional Halloween decor to transform your space into a dark forest crawling with creatures. The menu suggestions include a bevy of tasty treats fit for any Magizoologist, including Ron's Frightful Meatballs, The Monster Bowl of Monster Mix, and a sausage roll in the shape of the Basilisk. Guests can discover their Patronus with a fun party game or compete in the costume contest by taking their photo in the "Have You Seen This Wizard?" Photo Booth.

This Halloween, it's time for a trip into the Forbidden Forest. Keep an eye out for Grawp!

EVENT OVERVIEW

INVITATION
- A Magical Creatures Halloween Phoenix Invitation

DECORATIONS
- Forbidden Forest Balloon Backdrop
- Spider Legs
- Forbidden Forest Luminaries
- Wizarding World Directional Signs
- Nagini Pumpkin Snake

MENU SUGGESTIONS
- The Monster Book of Monster Mix
- Ron's Frightful Meatballs
- Defeating the Basilisk Sausage Roll
- Lumos Solem Salad
- The Cry of the Mandrake Cupcakes
- Mountain Troll Bogies
- Fawkes's Healing Tears
- Professor Lupin's Anti-Dementor Hot Chocolate

ACTIVITIES & FAVORS
- Discover Your Patronus Game & Favors
- "Have You Seen This Wizard?" Photo Booth & Costume Contest

A Magical Creatures Halloween Phoenix Invitation

Entice your guests to your Magical Creatures party with this gorgeous fold-out Phoenix Invitation. While these keepsake cards look intricate and complex, they're quite simple to create, and your guests will adore them.

- Phoenix Invitation template
- Electric cutting machine (Cricut) or scissors
- Cardstock
- Awl or other tool with a sharp point
- Small paper brads
- A7 envelopes

1. Download our Phoenix Invitation template from the online resources section.

2. If using a cutting machine like a Cricut, upload the SVG files to your design software. Fill in the details for your party. Print, then cut according to your machine's directions.

3. If using the PDF version, open the invitation in Adobe Reader. Fill in the details for your party in the editable fields. Print and cut it out with scissors.

4. Poke a small hole at each corner and on the tail area of the phoenix body. Poke a hole in the top of each wing and the top of the tail.

5. Attach wings and tail to the phoenix body with small brads.

6. Put each invitation into its envelope. Stamp your envelopes, address them, and put them the post

"FAWKES IS A PHOENIX, HARRY. THEY BURST INTO FLAME WHEN IT IS TIME FOR THEM TO DIE, AND THEN THEY ARE REBORN FROM THE ASHES."

Professor Dumbledore, *Harry Potter and the Chamber of Secrets*

YOU ARE INVITED TO A MAGICAL CREATURES HALLOWEEN PARTY

SATURDAY
OCTOBER 31ST

▶ 6 PM ◀

3 WHOMPING WILLOW LANE

RSVP

PROFESSOR LUPIN
310.101.3987

No Muggles Allowed

FORBIDDEN FOREST BALLOON BACKDROP

The showstopper craft for this Halloween party, this lush balloon backdrop will help you create the atmosphere of the Forbidden Forest right in your own home. You can go for a full balloon arch by using an arch kit ordered online or at your local party store, or create a backdrop using a low-tack tape like painter's tape to secure balloons to your wall. The addition of giant spider legs and faux tree branches completes the illusion!

- Balloons in Forbidden Forest colors (we used various shades of green and brown)
- Electric balloon inflator pump
- Plastic balloon arch decorating strip, to help form the arch (optional)
- Painter's tape
- Faux greenery such as branches and leaves
- Spider Legs (page 55)
- Plastic spiders and faux webbing (optional)

I. Inflate your balloons with various amounts of air to create variation in size. This will add visual interest to your arch or wall. An electric balloon inflator pump takes mere seconds to inflate each balloon and helps this step get done quickly.

2. Once you have your balloons ready, begin attaching them to the arch strip, if using one, or begin attaching to the wall with painter's tape. Make sure to stagger sizes to keep the wall looking interesting and not monotonous. Use painter's tape to attach some balloons to other balloons to fill in gaps.

3. Tuck faux greenery into balloons and attach with painter's tape to secure if necessary.

4. Tuck in spider legs and some webbing and faux spiders at various points to give the impression the legs are crawling out of the balloons.

SPIDER LEGS

Follow the spiders! The Acromantula in Harry Potter and the Chamber of Secrets *was a combination of practical and special effects. These creepy Acromantula legs, on the other hand, are made of simple kraft paper and spray paint. They're the perfect addition to your Forbidden Forest Balloon Arch, especially when paired with extra webbing and a few store-bought faux spiders for an extra creepy touch.*

• Scissors
• Brown kraft paper (on a roll)
• Black and gray spray paint

1. Cut kraft paper to desired length. We cut ours to 24 inches by 24 inches.

2. Roll paper into a long leg, and scrunch it as you roll to give it texture and help it hold its shape.

3. Spray-paint the legs black. Allow to dry.

4. Lightly spray with gray for extra dimension. Allow to dry.

5. Add to your balloon arch as shown on page 54.

BEHIND THE MAGIC

Aragog was designed using an aquatronic system that utilized cables pumped with water to create a smoother, more graceful movement. The spider's back legs were manipulated by puppeteers while his forelegs were mechanical and operated by a motion-control device called a waldo that reproduces movements made by a controller. The entire approach gave Aragog's movements an elegant yet menacing quality that mimicked the way real spiders creep around.

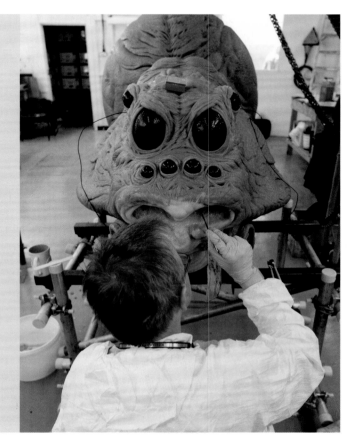

Forbidden Forest Luminaries

The Forbidden Forest is filled with a wide variety of creatures, some friendly, others not quite so much. These lanterns allow you to safely celebrate a few particular favorites, namely the centaurs, Buckbeak, and of course the Acromantula. Place a battery-operated candle inside to cast mysterious shadows throughout your party space. While a paper-cutting machine makes this craft a snap, we have also provided a PDF version you can cut out by hand.

- Forbidden Forest Luminary templates
- Electric cutting machine (Cricut) or scissors
- Pencil
- Black cardstock
- Vellum paper
- Double-sided tape or glue
- Battery-operated candle (one for each lantern)

1. Download our Forbidden Forest Luminary templates from the online resources section.

2. If using an electric paper cutter like a Cricut, upload the SVG files to your design software, and score and cut according to your machine's directions. (Make sure you add score lines to the folds.) Cut two sets of panels for each lantern.

3. If cutting by hand, download the PDF version and cut it out so that you have a pattern. Trace the pattern onto cardstock, and cut out the panels. As noted above, cut two sets of panels for each lantern.

4. Once the panels are cut, fold each panel.

5. Cut four strips of vellum for each lantern, and attach one piece to the inside of each panel using double-sided tape or glue.

6. Attach panels together with double-sided tape or glue.

7. Place the lantern over a battery-operated candle, and enjoy.

Behind the Magic

For *Harry Potter and the Order of the Phoenix*, the creature shop created two full-size models—called maquettes—of the centaurs Bane and Magorian that were used for cyberscanning into the computer. It took the costume and prop departments eight months and a crew of more than forty people to get from the initial sculpt of the centaurs to their final fittings with handcrafted weapons and jewelry.

NAGINI PUMPKIN SNAKE

The Harry Potter films are full of loyal and iconic companions, from Harry's beloved Hedwig to Voldemort's sinister Nagini. In this easy carving craft, create your very own Nagini—out of pumpkins! You can vary the length of your snake with the number of pumpkins you use. We recommend using a couple of pumpkin shapes to give extra interest to your creation. Using faux pumpkins will ensure you can use this creature year after year.

• Nagini template ◉
• Printer paper
• Scissors or X-acto knife
• Real or faux pumpkins (that can be carved)
• Pencil
• Pumpkin carving tools
• Battery-operated candles

1. Download the Nagini template from our online resources. Print out on normal printer and cut out the individual stencils using scissors or an X-acto knife.

2. Start by carving the face. Place the stencils on the pumpkin where you want to carve the face and trace them with pencil. Remove the stencils and carve the face details along the pencil lines.

3. Repeat this process with the scales stencils on the rest of your pumpkins.

4. Place pumpkins in a row, one behind the other, curving for interest. Have them "snake" up a set of steps for extra visual depth.

5. Place a battery-operated candle inside each pumpkin for a glowing effect.

"NAGINI . . . DINNER."

Lord Voldemort, *Harry Potter and the Deathly Hallows – Part 1*

Styling Magic!

The Forbidden Forest is seen in quite a few of the Harry Potter films, and production designer Stuart Craig considered it a character in and of itself. Originally shot on location in Black Park, Buckinghamshire, England for *Harry Potter and the Sorcerer's Stone*, a set for the forest was later constructed at Leavesden Studios and there it remained, growing and evolving with every consecutive film. The scale of the trees and their roots got bigger, the overall aesthetic became creepier and more frightening. By the fifth film, the trees were twelve to fourteen feet across—bigger than the redwoods in Northern California. In the eighth film, the painted cyclorama that served as the backdrop in scenes had grown to six hundred feet in length.

Use the Forbidden Forest Balloon Backdrop to anchor your party and create the color palette of the forest in your home. Instead of going with traditional black linens for a Halloween party, continue the forest theme with a deep green tablecloth and natural wood servingware. A bit of faux greenery tucked here and there will also help sell the forest effect. Your Forbidden Forest Luminaries can be used on the table, hanging from the ceiling, or lighting the path to the party, along with your Hogwarts Directional Sign and Nagini Pumpkin Craft. Tuck a few traditional Halloween decorations like jack-o'-lanterns and spider webbing here and there, and you are ready for a very spooky evening!

ABOVE: Harry and Draco serve detention in the Forbidden Forest in *Harry Potter and the Sorcerer's Stone*.

THE MONSTER BOOK OF MONSTER MIX

No party is complete without Monster Mix! Inspired by Hagrid's terrifying Care of Magical Creatures textbook from Harry Potter and the Prisoner of Azkaban, *this extravagant mix of sweet and savory nibbles features a spicy kick thanks to the pepper jelly glaze. For an eye-catching display, serve your Monster Mix in a crafted prop replica of the book from the film. Just be sure to watch your fingers!*

YIELD: APPROXIMATELY 10 CUPS

Cooking spray
One 11¾-ounce jar homemade or store-bought red pepper jelly
1 teaspoon kosher salt
1 teaspoon cayenne pepper
1 cup unsalted pecan halves
1 cup almonds
1 cup peanuts
1 cup pistachios, shells removed
1 cup pumpkin seeds
1 cup sunflower seeds
1 cup dried cranberries
1 cup shredded or flaked coconut
1 cup pretzels
1 cup yogurt-covered raisins

Preheat the oven to 350°F. Line a rimmed baking sheet with parchment paper. Spray with cooking spray, and set aside.

In a Dutch oven over medium heat, stir the pepper jelly with salt until the jelly melts. Once jelly is melted, turn off heat. Add cayenne pepper and nuts, stirring to coat nuts evenly.

Spread nuts out on prepared baking sheet, and roast in the oven for 10 minutes. Remove from the oven, stir, and allow to cook for another 10 minutes or until golden. Watch nuts carefully since ovens can vary; do not let them burn.

Remove pan from oven and carefully slide the parchment paper with nuts from the pan onto the counter to cool completely for approximately 15 minutes. This will help stop them continuing to brown on the hot pan.

Combine spiced nuts with seeds, dried cranberries, coconut, pretzels, and yogurt-covered raisins in a bowl. Transfer the mix to your serving dish and serve.

TIP

Want to make your own prop replica of the famous Care of Magical Creatures textbook? See The Monster Book of Monsters Prop Replica craft in *Harry Potter: Crafting Wizardry*.

Ron's Frightful Meatballs

Inspired by Ron's fear of spiders (Halloween is the time to celebrate your fears after all!), these delicious meatballs combine a unique Asian-inspired flavor profile with a creepy-crawly presentation that makes them the perfect addition to your spooktacular buffet table.

Yield: about 25 spiders

FOR THE DIPPING SAUCE

¼ cup soy sauce

2 tablespoons mirin

½ tablespoon chile paste or hot sauce

1 tablespoon honey

FOR THE MEATBALLS

½ cup tahini

3 to 5 drops black food coloring

1 tablespoon soy sauce

1 teaspoon fish sauce

2 tablespoons water

1 cup chow mein noodles, fried

1 pound bulk sausage

1 cup panko

2 tablespoons grated fresh ginger

¼ cup finely minced green onion, mostly white and light green

TO MAKE THE DIPPING SAUCE

Whisk all the ingredients together in a small bowl. Set aside until ready to serve.

TO MAKE THE MEATBALLS

Preheat the oven to 250°F, and line two rimmed baking sheets with parchment.

In a small bowl, whisk tahini, food coloring, soy sauce, and fish sauce together until well blended.

Mix two tablespoons of the above mixture with two tablespoons of water. In a medium bowl, toss the thinned sauce with one cup chow mein noodles. Spread the noodles out in an even layer onto a prepared baking sheet. Bake for 10 minutes and allow to cool completely. If baking the meatballs right away, raise oven temperature to 375°F. If not, turn off the oven.

Mix the remaining tahini mixture with the sausage, panko, ginger, and green onion.

Form the meatballs by scooping about 2 tablespoons of the mixture at a time, rolling into a ball, and inserting eight noodle "legs," four on each side. Set on prepared baking sheets. These can be made ahead and chilled up to 4 hours.

When ready to cook, preheat the oven to 375°F. Bake the meatballs for 15 minutes. Serve immediately with dipping sauce.

Defeating the Basilisk Sausage Roll

Any one of the magical creatures seen in the Harry Potter films is a combination of a wide variety of practical and special effects. But the Basilisk in Harry Potter and the Chamber of Secrets *is something special indeed. Originally intended to be created entirely through CGI, the creature shop eventually created a full-size sculpted puppet of the head and neck, which moved through aquatronics and cable controls. That Basilisk was made of foam latex stretched over aluminum, but to bring the King of Serpents to life in your kitchen, we recommend puff pastry.*

Yield: 6 to 8 servings

1½ pounds bulk pork sausage

½ cup fennel bulb and frond, minced

½ cup apple, peeled, cored, and minced

1 cup panko bread crumbs

1 tablespoon apple cider vinegar

Fresh ground black pepper

1 package puff pastry, defrosted according to package instructions

1 egg, lightly beaten with 1 tablespoon water, for egg wash

2 tablespoons Dijon mustard

¼ cup slivered almonds, chilled in the freezer for at least 20 minutes

1 red chile, such as a Fresno, or large piece of red bell pepper

Black olives, for garnish (optional)

Turmeric, for garnish (optional)

SPECIAL SUPPLIES

Kitchen shears

Prepare a baking sheet by lining with a silicone baking mat or parchment, and set aside.

In a medium bowl, combine the pork sausage, fennel, apple, panko, and vinegar. Season with pepper to taste. Cover in plastic wrap, and chill in the refrigerator for 1 hour.

While the sausage mixture is chilling, roll out each piece of puff pastry until it is approximately 15 inches in length.

Lay the puff pastry sheets out short end to short end, allowing them to overlap slightly. Brush the overlapping pieces of puff pastry with egg wash, and crimp with a fork to seal them together, creating one long piece. Cut the long piece in half, lengthwise, creating two long pieces: a top and a bottom.

Remove your sausage mixture from the refrigerator. Working with one piece of the puff pastry, form the sausage mixture into a roll covering the pastry end to end. Brush the edges of the puff pastry with egg wash and cover the sausage roll with the top piece. Fold the edges of the two pieces of pastry over each other, pinching them together to create a strong seam. The sausage roll should now be encased in a tube of pastry, possibly with some excess pastry on both ends.

Pinch one end of the pastry into a narrow point to form the tail. Starting at the tail end, use kitchen shears to make diagonal snips about a half-inch apart in both sides, all the way to the head on both side seams. This creates the Basilisk's side spikes.

Gently lift the Basilisk onto the prepared baking sheet, and arrange its body into snake-like curves so that it fits comfortably on the pan.

Using the shears again, trim any excess pastry away from the "head," and reserve the scraps. Shape the sausage into a mouth, just 2 or 3 inches deep. Line the mouth with the reserved pasty

scraps so all the sausage is covered, using egg wash to adhere it.

Insert the chile into the mouth. This will hold the mouth open while baking and create the Basilisk tongue. Poke slivered almonds into the mouth for fangs and on the head for spikes. Make eye indentations with your thumb on either side of the head. Use additional pastry scraps to create two eyeballs, egg wash them, and color them with turmeric if desired. Use toothpicks to adhere them to the head. Slices of olive can be added to create irises.

Preheat the oven to 425°F while you chill the sausage roll for 20 minutes. Bake for 30 to 40 minutes or until the puff pastry is a golden brown and the sausage temperature is 165°F. Serve immediately.

Continued on page 68

"OF THE MANY FEARSOME BEASTS THAT ROAM OUR LAND, NONE IS MORE DEADLY THAN THE BASILISK. CAPABLE OF LIVING FOR HUNDREDS OF YEARS, INSTANT DEATH AWAITS ANY WHO MEET THIS GIANT SERPENT'S EYE."

Harry Potter, reading from a torn page of a library book, *Harry Potter and the Chamber of Secrets*

ABOVE: Harry fights the Basilisk in *Harry Potter and the Chamber of Secrets*.

Making the Defeating the Basalisk Sausage Roll

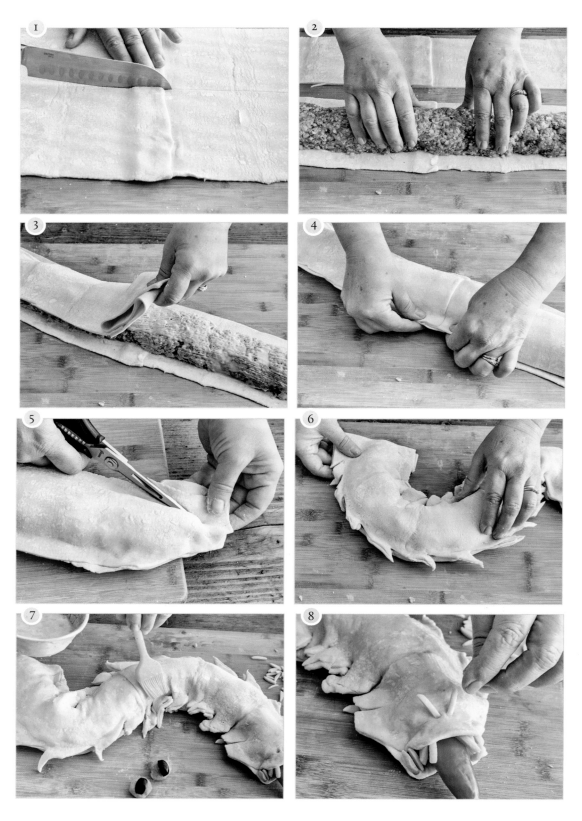

Lumos Solem Salad

Devil's Snare might hate sunlight but the bright and vivacious veggies in the delectable salad do not! A delicious combination of sunshine-loving summer vegetables, this healthy salad is inspired by the spell Lumos Solem, which produces a bright burst of sunlight that Hermione uses to defeat the Devil's Snare in Harry Potter and the Sorcerer's Stone.

YIELD: 6 TO 8 SERVINGS

FOR THE AVOCADO DRESSING

1 avocado
2 tablespoons apple cider vinegar
Juice of 1 lime
1 teaspoon salt, divided
⅓ cup olive oil
Fresh ground black pepper

FOR THE SALAD

1 teaspoon paprika
½ teaspoon salt
4 ears corn, shucked
2 tablespoon olive oil, divided
2 small bunches dinosaur kale, stemmed
1 large or 2 small cucumbers, peeled and seeded
3 stalks green onion, white and light green parts, thinly sliced
½ cup crumbled feta cheese

TO MAKE THE DRESSING

Puree the avocado, apple cider vinegar, lime juice, and ½ teaspoon of salt in a food processor until smooth, 1 to 2 minutes. Scrape down the sides of the bowl, and slowly add the olive oil while continuing to blend, until the dressing emulsifies. Add fresh ground pepper to taste.

TO MAKE THE SALAD

Preheat the oven to 400°F.

In a small bowl, combine paprika and salt. On a rimmed baking sheet, roll the shucked corn in 1 tablespoon of olive oil, and sprinkle with paprika-salt mixture.

Roast corn for 10 to 15 minutes or until kernels are fork tender. Allow to cool completely, about 20 minutes.

While corn is cooling, slice the kale into ribbons, and add to a medium bowl. Massage kale with remaining 1 tablespoon of olive oil and ½ teaspoon of salt. Set aside.

To remove the corn from the cob, stand a cob in a shallow bowl, holding it by its end. Use a knife to cut the kernels from the cob. Repeat with all the corn.

To assemble the salad, add the corn, cucumber, and green onion to the kale, and toss with the dressing. Add the feta, and toss again. Serve immediately or refrigerate up to 1 hour.

"DEVIL'S SNARE, DEVIL'S SNARE, IT'S DEADLY FUN . . . BUT WILL SULK IN THE SUN! THAT'S IT! DEVIL'S SNARE HATES SUNLIGHT!"

Hermione Granger, *Harry Potter and the Sorcerer's Stone*

THE CRY OF THE MANDRAKE CUPCAKES

Introduced in Harry Potter and the Chamber of Secrets, *Mandrakes are frankly unsightly plants whose roots appear in the shape of a baby capable of emitting a piercing, potentially deadly cry. Thankfully, no ear protection is required for these Baby Mandrake Cupcakes. Garden-friendly carrot cake is matched with a rich chocolate cream cheese frosting to simulate soil. We also added a few extra chocolate sprinkles for texture. The Mandrakes themselves are molded with fondant, with fresh mint leaves added for an extra touch of realism.*

YIELD: 12 CUPCAKES

FOR THE CUPCAKES

Cooking spray

1 cup all-purpose flour

½ cup granulated sugar

¼ cup light brown sugar

1 teaspoon ground cinnamon

¼ teaspoon grated nutmeg

¼ teaspoon ground ginger

1 teaspoon baking soda

½ teaspoon baking powder

¼ teaspoon salt

1½ cups grated carrots

⅔ cup canola oil

2 eggs, beaten

½ cup chopped pecans

FOR THE FROSTING

8 ounces cream cheese, softened to room temperature

½ cup unsalted butter, softened to room temperature

3½ cups powdered sugar

⅔ cup unsweetened cocoa powder

1 teaspoon pure vanilla extract

1 to 2 tablespoons half-and-half

Pinch of salt

FOR DECORATING

1 pound white fondant

Brown gel food coloring

Fresh mint sprigs

Chocolate sprinkles

SPECIAL SUPPLIES

Terra-cotta baking cups

Offset spatula

Toothpicks or wooden skewer, cut into small pieces

Continued on page 72

RIGHT: Concept Sketch of the Mandrake by Dermot Power for *Harry Potter and the Chamber of Secrets.*

TO MAKE THE CUPCAKES

Preheat the oven to 350°F. Lightly spray terra-cotta baking cups with cooking spray, and set aside.

In a large bowl, combine the flour, sugars, cinnamon, nutmeg, ginger, baking soda, baking powder, and salt.

Combine the grated carrots and the oil in a separate medium bowl. Slowly add the carrots to the flour mixture, stirring until just mixed. Add the eggs and pecans, and gently stir to combine, being careful not to overmix.

Spoon the batter into the prepared baking cups, filling each approximately two-thirds full.

Bake for 12 to 14 minutes or until cooked through and a toothpick comes out clean.

Allow to cool completely before frosting.

TO MAKE THE FROSTING

In the bowl of a stand mixer fitted with a paddle attachment, beat cream cheese and butter on medium speed for 1 minute until completely smooth and creamy.

Add in powdered sugar, cocoa powder, vanilla, 1 tablespoon of half-and-half, and salt, and beat until creamy.

Add more half-and-half if you need to thin the frosting.

Using an offset spatula, apply a thin to medium layer of frosting to the cooled cupcakes.

TO MAKE THE MANDRAKES

Add a couple of drops of gel food coloring to your fondant, and begin to knead the fondant to blend the color throughout. Add more coloring as needed to achieve your desired color. Note: Gel food coloring is intense, so a little goes a long way. We recommend you start light and add more if needed.

Once you have the color you desire, divide the fondant into 12 pieces, approximately 3 inches by 4 inches, one for each of your Mandrakes (you may have some fondant leftover). Working with one Mandrake at a time, tear a third of the fondant off and reserve it for the head. Tear another small amount from your remaining fondant, and reserve this for the arms and roots.

With the remaining large piece of fondant, begin to roll and shape it into the Mandrake body, a roundish triangle with the wide part at the bottom. Press the bottom onto your surface so that you give your mandrake a good base to sit on. Set aside.

Roll the headpiece into a ball, and adhere to the body with a toothpick or short piece of wooden skewer. Pull some "roots" up from the head and use a toothpick or skewer to create the eyes, mouth, and body texture. Poke a hole in the back of the head for the mint and two holes in the side of the body for the arms.

Roll the remaining piece into a long snake-like shape, and break it into four to five pieces so that you have two arms and a few pieces of roots to attach.

Connect the arms to the Mandrake, pinching to join the fondant pieces together. Wait to add the roots until the Mandrake is on the cupcake.

Sprinkle the top of each cupcake with chocolate jimmies. Alternatively, you can pour the jimmies onto a plate and dip the top of each iced cupcake into them to create a smooth layer of sprinkles over the icing.

Place the Mandrake on top of the iced cupcake. If your Mandrake needs a little extra support, place a toothpick behind it in the cake to help stabilize it. Add the remaining roots to the base of the Mandrake and a sprig of fresh mint to the Mandrake head where you placed the hole.

Repeat with the rest of the cupcakes and serve.

BEHIND THE MAGIC

More than fifty completely mechanical Mandrakes were created that made up the top halves of their flowerpots, their movement achieved by one of the most basic special-effects techniques—animatronic puppetry. The machinery for the Mandrakes was inside the pots, operated underneath the greenhouse table by controllers.

TOP: Hermione pulls a Mandrake out of its pot. ABOVE: The Gryffindor Second Years attend a lesson on Mandrakes in the Hogwarts Greenhouses in *Harry Potter and the Chamber of Secrets*.

Mountain Troll Bogies

Nothing brings friends together quite like battling a mountain troll—as Harry, Ron, and Hermione discover in a pivotal scene from Harry Potter and the Sorcerer's Stone. *Inspired by the sticky end to that tricky situation, this bogey-colored party treat may sound gruesome, but it's actually quite delicious. Dare your guests to take on the troll with this salty-sweet popcorn snack.*

Yield: 10 to 12 servings (16 cups)

½ cup popcorn kernels, popped,
or approximately 16 cups popcorn

1 cup pepitas

1 cup plus 2 tablespoons (2¼ sticks)
unsalted butter, divided

2 teaspoons kosher salt

1 cup plus 1 tablespoon sugar, divided

¼ cup light corn syrup

½ teaspoon vanilla extract

Green food coloring

1 teaspoon baking soda

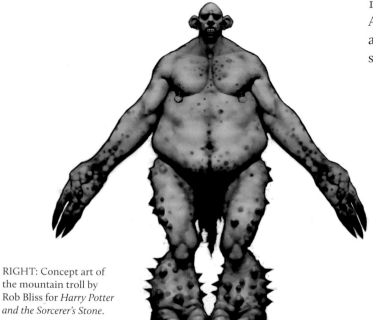

RIGHT: Concept art of
the mountain troll by
Rob Bliss for *Harry Potter
and the Sorcerer's Stone.*

Preheat the oven to 250°F, and line two baking sheets with parchment. Pour the popcorn into a large, heatproof bowl and have on hand.

Heat a large dry skillet over high heat until it is very hot. Add the pepitas, turn down the heat to medium, and toast 2 to 3 minutes until fragrant. Set aside.

Melt the butter with the sugar and light corn syrup in a medium saucepan over medium-high heat. Bring to a boil, stirring constantly. Once everything is melted and the mixture is at a rolling boil, boil for 4 minutes without stirring, and then remove from heat. Add in vanilla, salt, green food coloring, and baking soda. The baking soda will make the mixture foam and bubble—this is normal! Once the foam has died down, add the pepitas and stir to combine.

Pour the mixture over the popcorn, and mix until all the popcorn is thoroughly coated.

Pour onto prepared baking sheets, and bake for 1 hour, stirring and turning every 15 minutes. Allow to cool for 5 minutes, and then break up and store in an airtight container. This can be stored up to a week.

"Troll in the dungeon! Thought
you ought to know."

Professor Quirrell, *Harry Potter and the Sorcerer's Stone*

Fawkes's Healing Tears

At the end of Harry Potter and the Chamber of Secrets, *Harry heroically defeats the Basilisk with the Sword of Gryffindor, but not before the snake manages to inflict a fatal wound in his upper arm. It is Fawkes the Phoenix who saves Harry's life, using his healing tears to counteract the venom and close the wound. Inspired by Fawkes's tears, this sparkly drink may not have quite the same healing power, but it is still a refreshing drink to keep you on your toes and ready for your next challenge. Note: We recommend you chill your ingredients before mixing and serve this immediately while the soda is most bubbly.*

YIELD: 8 SERVINGS

16 ounces orange juice, chilled

16 ounces cranberry-peach juice, chilled

32 ounces lemon-lime soda, chilled

Blood orange slices, for garnish

White luster dust, for garnish

Combine juices and soda, and in a large pitcher or punch bowl. Garnish with blood orange slices and luster dust. Set out with glasses in an area where guests can serve themselves.

BEHIND THE MAGIC

The Fawkes we see in the movie was an audio-animatronic bird who could perform a number of actions. He could move his weight around, the way birds do when they walk, open his wings, raise his crest, blink, create all sorts of small facial expressions, and even cry "real" tears. Fawkes was so lifelike, in fact, that at one point, actor Richard Harris, who played Dumbledore in the first two movies, thought he was a real bird!

PROFESSOR LUPIN'S ANTI-DEMENTOR HOT CHOCOLATE

First introduced in Harry Potter and the Prisoner of Azkaban, *Dementors are dark creatures that suck the happiness out of those around them. They are, according to Professor Lupin, "among the foulest creatures to walk the earth." Fortunately, the effects of an encounter with a Dementor can be easily counteracted with a simple remedy: chocolate! Featuring a heaping helping of cocoa powder and two types of chocolate—one for the cocoa and one for the whipped cream—this rich and creamy drink is the perfect restorative for any bad day. Be sure to have plenty on hand at your party to help guests celebrate finishing the Discover Your Patronus game!*

Yield: 4 servings

FOR THE WHIPPED CREAM

2 ounces white chocolate
½ cup mini marshmallows
½ cup heavy cream

FOR THE HOT CHOCOLATE

¼ cup unsweetened cocoa powder
½ cup sugar
Pinch of salt
⅓ cup water
½ cup heavy cream
2 ounces dark chocolate
3 cups milk
Chocolate bars, for garnish (optional)

TO MAKE THE WHIPPED CREAM

In a microwave-safe bowl, heat the white chocolate for 30 seconds. Stir until melted, and fold in the marshmallows. Set aside.

In a large bowl of a stand mixer fitted with the whisk attachment, whip the cream on high speed until stiff peaks form, 2 to 3 minutes.

Fold in chocolate-marshmallow mixture, and refrigerate until needed.

TO MAKE THE HOT CHOCOLATE

Combine the cocoa, sugar, salt, and water in a medium saucepan over medium-high heat. Bring to a boil, stirring constantly until sugar is completely dissolved.

Turn down heat to medium-low, and stir in half a cup of cream until smooth. Remove from heat, and set aside.

Melt the dark chocolate in the microwave as you did the white chocolate, and use a pastry brush to swipe swaths of chocolate on the insides of each glass. Set aside.

In a large saucepan, heat the milk until just before boiling. Remove from heat.

Divide the cocoa-cream mixture among the four glasses. Fill each about two thirds of the way full with the hot milk.

Pipe or scoop a big dollop of the whipped cream mixture on the top, garnish with chocolate bars, if using, and enjoy.

DISCOVER YOUR PATRONUS GAME & FAVORS

A Patronus is a potent magical force that acts as a shield for the witch or wizard that conjures it, taking the form of an animal that they have a special connection to. First appearing in Harry Potter and the Prisoner of Azkaban, *they are primarily used to defend against Dementors, dark creatures which happen to be Harry's greatest fear, as he learns the first time he is confronted with a Boggart. Now guests can discover their Patronus with this fun party game, which features DIY Patronus Figurines in black bags tied to shrouded balloons symbolizing the Dementors. Guests can use the Patronus Charm and their wand to battle (pop) the Dementors and reveal their Patronus! Be sure to have a few mugs of Professor Lupin's Anti-Dementor Hot Chocolate on hand for when you're done!*

NOTE: It is suggested to have the host or helper monitor this game, especially if there are children present, as it requires something sharp to pop the Dementor balloons. Children should never be allowed to use sharp elements without adult supervision.

FOR THE PATRONUS FIGURINE

- Old newspaper, for work surface
- Silver spray paint
- Small plastic animal figurines

FOR THE DEMENTORS

- Small kraft bags, one per guest
- Small hole punch
- Black Halloween cloth
- Black balloons with long black ribbon (one per Dementor)
- Tissue paper confetti (optional)
- Scissors
- Nylon fishing string
- Tape
- Wand
- Hat pin
- Glue dot

TO MAKE THE PATRONUS FIGURINES

Working outside on a surface covered with newspaper, spray an even coat of silver spray paint on one side of the desired number of plastic animal figures, ensuring each animal is completely covered. When the figures are dry, flip them over, and spray an even coat on the other side. Let them dry fully for a day or two.

TO MAKE THE DISCOVER YOUR PATRONUS GAME

Place one Patronus figure in the bottom of a small kraft bag. Fold over the top of the bag, and hole-punch a space for the balloon ribbon. Set the finished bags aside while you prepare the Dementor balloons.

Fill each balloon with tissue paper confetti, if using, and blow them up. Blowing them up with helium will make the next step easier, however normal air will work as well.

Drape the black Halloween cloth over the balloons to the desired length. Cut the cloth at different lengths, draping off the balloon to give it that real Dementor look! Note: This step is much easier with two people. One person can hold the balloon steady while the other person drapes and cuts the cloth.

Continued on page 81

Tape a piece of fishing wire to the top center of each balloon. Hang the balloons from the ceiling at different heights to give the look of hovering Dementors!

Attach each of the balloon ribbons to a bag with a Patronus in it.

TO PLAY THE GAME

Attach a hat pin to the end of a wand with a glue dot. Have an adult monitor the game and hand the wand to players one at a time so they can dispatch their Dementor. Always take the wand back immediately after the player is finished using it.

Players choose a Dementor from the game and use the Patronus charm to defeat it, popping the balloon with the wand. Once they are "safe," they will then open the attached bag to discover their unique Patronus that helped keep them safe during their attack.

BEHIND THE MAGIC

To create the Dementors for the film, designers referenced embalmed bodies, whose wrappings were rotting and falling off, and added overlaid textures to give the appearance of decay.

"Have You Seen This Wizard?" Photo Booth & Costume Contest

Set up a snapshot photo station to take pics of guests. Allow them to vote on their favorites by hanging images on the wall and asking guests to add a tally mark to each of their favorites. The photo with the most votes wins!

FOR THE PHOTO FRAME

- "Have You Seen This Wizard?" photo frame template ⊙
- 22-by-28-inch poster board
- Pencil
- Scissors
- X-acto knife
- Double-sided tape or glue

FOR THE PHOTO BOOTH

- Backdrop of your choice
- Instant camera
- Photo props of your choice
- Foraged tree branch or stick
- Twine
- Clothespins
- Pens and paper

TO MAKE THE PHOTO FRAME

1. Download our "Have You Seen This Wizard?" photo frame template from our online resources.

2. The backdrop is sized to print on one poster board. We recommend printing this through your favorite local print shop on nice cardstock.

3. Once printed, use scissors to cut out the center section of the cardstock so that you have a frame. Place this over your poster board, and trace the inner frame onto the poster board with pencil.

4. Use scissor and/or an X-acto knife to cut through the poster board along the pencil line, removing the center section to match the printed poster.

5. Attach the "Have You Seen This Wizard?" photo frame poster to the poster board with double-sided tape or glue.

BEHIND THE MAGIC

Wanted posters were created for a number of characters throughout the films, from Lucius Malfoy to Fenrir Greyback to Harry Potter himself. The one featuring the now iconic "Have You Seen This Wizard?" design was originally created for Sirius Black in *Harry Potter and the Prisoner of Azkaban*. Two versions of this poster were created for filming: a "flat version" containing a still photo and text and a version with a green screen in place of the photo so the moving footage of actor Gary Oldman could be added in postproduction.

TO SET UP YOUR PHOTO BOOTH

6. Set up a backdrop of your choice in a well-lit area away from any well-trafficked paths or hubs (you don't want people walking into your photos). Set the "Have You Seen This Wizard?" photo frame against the backdrop and set up a table with an instant camera and any extra props you want to include.

7. Attach several lengths of twine to a slender, sturdy tree branch. Hang the branch nearby, and set a jar of clothespins next to it.

8. Guests can take pictures of each other in their Halloween costumes using the frame and props. Attach the pictures with clothespins to the twine once they've developed.

9. To turn this into a costume contest, have guests add a tally to the bottom of each photo they want to vote for or on a nearby piece of paper. The photo with the most votes wins!

Back to Hogwarts Movie Marathon

"Excuse me, sir, can you tell me where
I might find platform 9¾?"

Harry Potter, *Harry Potter and the Sorcerer's Stone*

Back to Hogwarts Movie Marathon

What's the best way to relive all the magic of the Harry Potter films? By hosting a movie marathon, of course! Whether you want to start from the beginning with *Harry Potter and the Sorcerer's Stone*, relive the Triwizard Tournament with *Harry Potter and the Goblet of Fire*, or jump straight into the wizarding war with *Harry Potter and the Half-Blood Prince*, this casual, cozy party will help you set the mood for hours of magical fun.

The theme of this party is, appropriately, "Back to Hogwarts," with a special focus on the Hogwarts Express and Platform 9¾. The menu suggestions are designed for a relaxed evening of snacking, with a focus on finger foods of both the sweet and savory variety. This includes a trio of popcorns, hearty Hogwarts First Years' Zucchini Boats, sweet Flying Broomstick Cake Pops, and a fizzy float inspired by the luxurious Prefects' bathroom. The entryway to the party provides an opportunity for some fun crafting as you create your own version of the entrance to Platform 9¾, and we encourage you to decorate the rest of the room with trunks, trolleys, and other props that connect to the iconic train. To make your movie watching even more fun and interactive, we've created a Harry Potter Bingo game, which should keep your guests on their toes.

Are you ready to travel back to Hogwarts? Got your ticket? Then all aboard!

Event Overview

INVITATION
- Letter from Hogwarts Party Invitation With Platform 9¾ Ticket

DECORATIONS
- Platform 9¾ Sign
- Platform 9¾ Brick Backdrop
- Honeydukes Trolley Sign

MENU SUGGESTIONS
- Hogwarts First Years' Zucchini Boats
- Weasleys' Wizard Wheezes Teeth-Sealing Popcorn
- Hogwarts Express Smokey Sliders
- Hungarian Horntail Hot Wings
- Flying Broomstick Cake Pops
- Prefect Fizzy Floats

ACTIVITIES
- Harry Potter Bingo
- Harry Potter Temporary Tattoos

FAVORS
- Chocolate Frogs

Letter From Hogwarts Party Invitation With Platform 9¾ Ticket

Most trips to Hogwarts usually begin with a letter! These keepsake party invitations are based on Harry's own letter from Hogwarts and come with an official Hogwarts Express ticket to gain entrance to the party.

- Letter from Hogwarts Party Invitation template ⬇
- White 8.5-by-11-inch printer paper
- Cover weight paper, 65–80 pound
- Scissors
- Glue

1. Download the Letter from Hogwarts Party Invitation template from our online resources. This will include the letter, which serves as the invitation, the envelope, and the Hogwarts Express ticket.

2. Open the letter in Adobe Reader. Fill in the details for your party in the editable fields.

3. Print the letter on printer paper, then turn the paper over, and print the back of the letter if desired (it adds to the authenticity!).

4. Open the envelope in Adobe Reader. Fill in your guests' address details in the editable fields.

5. Print the envelopes on cover weight paper and cut them out.

6. Open the Hogwarts Express ticket. Print on printer paper and cut out.

7. Fold the envelopes along the fold lines and use glue to seal the edges. Fold the letter into thirds, and place the folded letter and ticket inside the envelope.

8. Stamp your envelopes, address them, and put them the post!

BACK TO HOGWARTS

We are pleased to inform you that you have been
back to Hogwarts School of Witchcraft and W
for
a Harry Potter Movie Marathon
on
Saturday, September 24
at 6 pm

Please find enclosed your ticket for the Ho
Express. All students are required to bring
for admittance

Please arrive dressed in your hous

Report to Platform
located at
1 Hogwarts Way

RSVP by Owl Post
Professor McGonagall
Gryffindor House, Hogwarts

HOGWARTS

LONDON TO
Platform

R. H. POTTER
The Cupboard under the Stairs
4 Privet Drive
Little Whinging
SURREY

PLATFORM 9¾ SIGN

Style the entrance to your party to look like the entrance to Platform 9¾, complete with a sign based on the real set piece from the film.

FOR THE FRAME

- 10-by-25-inch used frame (or make your own)
- Miter saw (optional)
- Wood Glue (optional)
- 10-by-25-inch particle board (optional)
- Painter's tape
- Craft paint in red, brown, or mixture of both

FOR THE SIGN

- Hogwarts Express Sign template ⬇
- Electric cutting machine such as a Cricut
- Black and gold vinyl
- Transfer paper
- Rubbing tool or craft stick
- Scissors
- Foam brush
- White paint
- Paintbrush
- 9¾ Symbol template ⬇
- Matte-finish Mod Podge or craft glue substitute

TIP

Always use caution when working with saws and other electric tools and wear appropriate safety gear including protective eyewear.

ABOVE: Mrs. Weasley tells Harry how to get to Platform 9¾ in *Harry Potter and the Sorcerer's Stone.*

TO MAKE THE FRAME

1. Find a thrift store frame that is long and skinny, preferably one that already has a stained wood frame. If not, create your own frame by using a miter saw to cut 45 degree angles on two 25-inch and two 10-inch pieces cut from 2-by-1-inch wood. Glue the long and short sides together at angle-cut corners, and add particle board back.

2. Put painter's tape over the frame edge, and paint the backboard with craft paint. You want to achieve a reddish brown color, which may require some mixing.

3. Remove the painter's tape from the frame while paint is still wet. Allow it to dry for a few hours.

TO CREATE THE SIGN

4. Download the Hogwarts Express Sign template from our online resources.

5. Upload the text for the sign to your cutting machine's design software, and cut out in gold vinyl according to machine and material directions.

6. Weed the excess vinyl from your design, and place transfer paper over the image. Use your hand or a credit card to firmly press the transfer paper to your design to ensure it's sticking well, then gently peel the paper away from the original vinyl backing so the text adheres to the transfer paper. Apply the cut vinyl design to the red backboard, and rub it on using a rubbing tool or craft stick. Remove the transfer paper.

7. Create a circle stencil by tracing a 4-inch circle on a 6-inch square scrap of black vinyl. Clip a hole in the center of the circle you traced, and cut along your traced line using scissors. This will create a square with a circle cut out of the middle to use as a stencil. Alternatively, you can create this on the cutting machine with vinyl.

8. Place the vinyl stencil above the Hogwarts Express words, and rub it onto the wood using a rubbing tool, making sure to rub the edges of the circle carefully so the paint doesn't bleed through. Using a foam brush, paint the inside of the circle white. Wait about an hour, and do a second coat to make sure the circle is completely white. Remove the vinyl stencil. If any paint bled through, touch up the edges with some of the reddish-brown paint you used above.

9. Download the 9¾ Symbol template from our online resources.

10. Upload the symbol to your cutting machine's design software, and cut out in black vinyl according to machine and material directions.

11. Weed the excess vinyl from your design, and place transfer paper over the symbol. Use your hand or a credit card to firmly press the transfer paper to your design to ensure it's sticking well, then gently peel the paper away from the original vinyl backing so the symbol adheres to the transfer paper. Apply the cut vinyl symbol onto the white circle, and rub it on using a rubbing tool or craft stick. Remove the transfer paper.

12. Paint matte finish Mod Podge on the entire sign, and allow a few hours to dry.

PLATFORM 9¾ BRICK BACKDROP

As Harry learns in Harry Potter and the Sorcerer's Stone, *the only way to get to Platform 9¾ is to walk straight through the barrier separating platforms nine and ten. The famous film moment is easily replicated with this simple painting craft, which turns a simple bedsheet into the gateway to an epic adventure.*

- Drop cloth or disposable plastic tablecloth
- Taupe twin sheet
- 2 or 3 large sponges
- Scissors
- Different colors of paint (we used taupe, brown, pink, peach)
- Paint tray liners
- Extendable tension rod

1. Lay a plastic tablecloth or drop cloth down to protect the floor before you begin painting. For best results, set this up outside where there's no risk of getting paint on nice floors or furniture.

2. Lay the twin sheet vertically on top of the drop cloth in front of you, and prep your paint supplies.

3. Take large sponges and cut them in half. This will give them a more brick-like look while painting.

4. Pour a little of each color into paint tray liners. To create the look of the King's Cross Station brick wall, the paint colors should be taupe, brown, pink, and peach. Don't forget to use liners for quick and easy clean up!

5. Press the sponge into the paint, then apply it to the top left corner of the sheet to make a spongy, brick-like rectangle. Return the sponge to the paint to re-wet it. You can use the same color, a different color, or a mix of two (real bricks have a lots of varied colors in them). Sponge a second brick right next to the first one, leaving a half-inch gap between the two to function as the grout line. Repeat this process, varying your colors until you've reached the end of the row. Then start your second row about a half-inch below the first, shifting the bricks about a half a brick to the left so the grout lines don't line up perfectly.

6. As you paint, start to ombré the colors to get darker shades by the bottom third of the sheet.

7. Once you get to the bottom of the sheet, go back through and add in any half or quarter bricks to the sides of the sheet where there's empty space.

8. Let the paint dry completely before hanging the sheet.

9. Once the painted sheet is completely dry, take a pair of scissors and cut a straight line up the center of the twin sheet, but do not cut it all the way. You want to leave about a foot uncut at the top to keep the wall coming back together once a guest walks through it.

10. Prepare your brick wall for easy hanging by cutting the sides of the top of the sheet. There is a natural pocket where you can slide a tension rod through a sheet if you simply trim off the sides of the top of the sheet.

11. Slide the tension rod through the pocket at the top of the sheet for easy hanging in any doorway. Or, instead of using a tension rod, you could feed some rope through to tie around something.

12. Hang your sheet in the entryway to the party, and set up the sign next to it. Guests will have to walk through the wall to King's Cross Station to board the Hogwarts Express!

Honeydukes Trolley Sign

"Anything off the trolley dears?" Style your own version of the Honeydukes trolley to create a tempting food cart for guests to sample throughout the evening. Top it off with this colorful Honeydukes sign, based on the official logo created by graphic artists Miraphora Mina and Eduardo Lima.

- Honeydukes logo printable ⬇
- Cardstock
- Scissors
- Pencil
- 10-by-30-by-¾-inch wood board
- Safety goggles
- Circular saw or jigsaw
- 200-grit sandpaper
- Four 5-gallon paint sticks for trim
- Miter saw
- Wood stain in dark walnut
- Paper towels
- Mod Podge or craft glue substitute
- Liquid Nails
- 2 eye sockets
- 3- to 4-foot black small-link chain

1. Download the Honeydukes logo printable from our online resources, and take to your local print shop to have it printed on cardstock. The finished sign is 28½ inches by 11½ inches. You can either print this as one large sign, or have them print each half on 12-by-18-inch paper and attach them to make one piece. Use scissors to cut out the logo so the entire sign is in the shape of a diamond.

2. With a pencil, trace the edge of your diamond-shaped cardstock logo onto your wood board. Set the cardstock logo aside. Using a circular saw or jigsaw, cut the traced shape out of the wood. Make sure to wear safety goggles, and follow the manufacturer's instructions.

3. Sand the edges of the wood sign until smooth.

4. Lay the trim pieces against the edges of the diamond-shaped sign. The trim pieces should be standing upright so they are taller than the surface of the sign. It will look like you are framing the diamond with about three-quarters of an inch of the trim piece exposed next to the wood. Using a pencil, mark the correct length to cut trim pieces.

5. Cut the trim pieces using a saw. This is easiest with a miter saw, because it has preset angles. To create perfect angles for each corner, the top and bottom angles will be close to 60 degrees, and the two sides will be close to 120 degrees.

6. Stain all pieces with a dark stain. Wipe off stain with a paper towel, and let dry for at least an hour.

Continued on page 96

LEFT: Wizarding sweets labels designed by Miraphora Mina and Eduardo Lima.

7. Attach the logo to the board by painting the front with Mod Podge and then laying the cardstock logo on top. Let dry for an hour or two, then gently sand off any overhang.

8. Attach the trim pieces to the edges of the sign using Liquid Nails. You can also use finishing nails, but the liquid make it easier to adjust the edges to match. Let dry about an hour.

9. If any of the pointed edges don't match up well, sand down and restain those edges.

10. Paint the entire sign in Mod Podge or craft glue substitute. Let dry overnight.

11. Attach eye sockets to the top of the frame, about 6 inches from the top point in both directions (one to the left and one to the right), and hang with the chain.

Styling Magic!

The set design for the interior compartments of the Hogwarts Express was inspired by one of director Chris Columbus's favorite movies, *A Hard Day's Night*, starring The Beatles. He wanted it to look exactly like the train the band travels in at the beginning of the movie, and production designer Stuart Craig was happy to oblige.

Styling this party is all about getting cozy, so make sure you have lots of pillows and blankets on hand so everyone can be warm and comfortable. Trunks make excellent props for this party and can often be found at thrift stores, garage sales, or antique shops. Use a couple trunks to style the entryway to the party, and use one as a coffee table. Another key piece of décor is your trolley. This can be something you craft to look exactly like the Honeydukes Trolley from the films, or you can simply take an existing cart and style it with jars of Harry Potter treats, your Chocolate Frog favors, and other small pieces of ephemera.

ABOVE: Ron and Hermione (and Crookshanks) in one of the Hogwarts Express compartments in *Harry Potter and the Prisoner of Azkaban*.

Hogwarts First Years' Zucchini Boats

As we see in Harry Potter and the Sorcerer's Stone, *first-year students get their first awe-inspiring sight of Hogwarts castle from a small fleet of boats led across the Black Lake by Hagrid. Inspired by that iconic moment, these delicious zucchini boats are filled with sausage, cheese, and pepperoni. An easy, low-carb dish you can keep as a side or turn into an entrée, these boats can (and should!) be arranged in the shape of the small Hogwarts flotilla, ferrying students to school for the first time.*

Yield: 8 boats

4 large zucchini
1 pound bulk Italian sausage
1 tablespoon olive oil
½ large onion, diced
Salt and fresh ground black pepper
1 cup shredded mozzarella cheese
½ cup pepperoni slices

Preheat the oven to 375°F.

Slice each zucchini in half lengthwise. Use a spoon to scoop out some of the pulp, leaving about half an inch of flesh for stability. Reserve pulp.

Heat oil in an a large sauté pan over medium heat. Cook sausage and onion until sausage is brown, 7 to 10 minutes. Add reserved zucchini pulp to the pan with the sausage and onion. Continue cooking until sausage is cooked through and onions are translucent, 5 to 7 minutes. Season with salt and pepper to taste.

Place the zucchini boats on a baking sheet lined with parchment paper. Divide the sausage and onion mix evenly among the boats. Top with shredded mozzarella cheese and finish with pepperoni slices.

Bake 20 minutes for firm boats, longer if you want the zucchini to be softer.

Arrange the boats on a serving board in the shape of the Hogwarts flotilla. Serve hot.

Weasleys' Wizard Wheezes Teeth-Sealing Popcorn

In Harry Potter and the Half-Blood Prince, *we get an up-close look at Fred and George Weasley's new joke shop, Weasley's Wizard Wheezes. The bustling shop is packed with colorful merchandise, including a giant popcorn machine, which we briefly see at the very end of the scene. While we never see exactly what kind of popcorn comes out of that machine, we can assume the inventors of the Puking Pastille wouldn't sell ordinary popcorn. Inspired by their creativity, we bring you Weasleys' Wizard Wheezes Teeth-Sealing Popcorn, coated with enough caramel to literally seal your teeth together. It's a perfectly delicious way to keep people from talking during the movie.*

Yield: 6 cups

1 tablespoon canola oil
¼ cup popcorn, unpopped
1 cup (2 sticks) butter
1 cup brown sugar
2 teaspoons vanilla extract
½ teaspoon baking soda
1 cup chocolate chips
1 teaspoon coconut oil
Popcorn salt

Place canola oil in a Dutch oven over medium-low heat. Place two to three kernels of unpopped popcorn in the pan as "test poppers." Once the kernels in the pan pop, add the remaining kernels. Cover and lightly shake pan to help distribute the kernels. Continue to periodically shake the pan until all kernels are popped or the popping sound slows to 2 to 3 seconds between pops. Remove from the heat, and set aside.

Melt butter in a medium saucepan over medium heat, and add brown sugar, stirring continuously. Bring to a boil, and allow it to boil for 4 minutes without stirring.

At the 4-minute mark, stir in vanilla, and allow to boil for 1 minute longer. Stir in the baking soda. Pour the caramel over popcorn, stirring to evenly coat all the kernels, until the popcorn is well-coated (you may not need to use all the caramel).

Place chocolate chips and coconut oil in a microwave-safe bowl, and heat for 30 seconds. Stir and continue to heat in 10-second increments if necessary until the chocolate is completely melted.

Pour chocolate over caramel popcorn, and serve immediately.

Hogwarts Express
Smokey Sliders

The Hogwarts Express appears in each of the Harry Potter films, traveling from King's Cross Station in London to Hogsmeade and back again with a trainful of young wizards and witches off to begin their magical studies. To create the Hogwarts Express, the filmmakers rescued and restored an abandoned steam locomotive named Olton Hall from a South Wales scrapyard. Inspired by the billowing smoke of the Hogwarts Express, these sliders have a delicious, smoky flavor profile and make a great main dish or appetizer, depending on how many passengers you're serving.

YIELD: 6 SERVINGS AS AN ENTREE; 12 OR MORE AS AN APPETIZER

FOR THE ROASTED RED PEPPER MAYO

1 cup mayonnaise

½ cup minced roasted red bell pepper

½ teaspoon smoked paprika

½ teaspoon ancho chile powder

¼ teaspoon cayenne pepper

FOR THE PATTIES

2 pounds ground beef

1 pound sliced bacon, divided

1 cup shredded Gouda (about a 3-ounce block)

1 teaspoon kosher salt

1 teaspoon smoked paprika

1 tablespoon ketchup

FOR THE SLIDERS

24 slider rolls, preferably "brown and serve" style

¼ cup (½ stick) butter, melted

½ teaspoon ancho chile powder

2 tablespoons poppy seeds

6 small tomatoes, as close to the bun size as possible

TO MAKE THE ROASTED RED PEPPER MAYO

In a small bowl, combine all the ingredients, and chill until needed.

TO MAKE THE PATTIES

Preheat the oven to 400°F. Lay out the bacon in a single layer on a baking sheet lined with foil or parchment, and cook until crisp, 12 to 15 minutes. Transfer to a paper-towel-lined plate, and allow to cool completely. Break off 24 slider-sized pieces, about 2 inches, and set aside.

Chop the rest of the bacon until fine. In a large bowl, mix the chopped bacon with the ground beef, shredded Gouda, salt, paprika, and ketchup.

Place the buns on a baking sheet. Mix the melted butter with the ancho chile powder, and brush the tops and sides of each bun. Sprinkle with poppy seeds. Bake for 6 to 8 minutes or until golden brown. Remove from the oven, and set aside.

Place a clean rimmed baking sheet in the oven, and raise the temperature to 425°F.

On a cookie sheet lined with parchment, divide the meat mixture into 24 even balls. Gently smash them with a small glass to form patties, about 2 to 2½ inches in diameter. Transfer the sliders on their parchment to the heated baking sheet.

Continued on page 104

While the patties are cooking, slice the tomatoes thinly, and set aside.

Cook the patties for 4 minutes, then turn them over. Place a piece of the reserved bacon on each patty, and cook another 3 to 5 minutes until cooked through.

TO ASSEMBLE THE SLIDERS

Put about a teaspoon of the pepper mayo on each bun bottom and top. Place a slice of tomato on each bottom, top with a patty, and then a second slice of tomato. Place a bun top on each slider. Secure with a cocktail pick if desired.

฿EHIND THE ΜAGIC

The Platform 9¾ scene in *Harry Potter and the Sorcerer's Stone* was filmed on a Sunday afternoon at London's King's Cross station, a slightly less busy time for the otherwise bustling station. Wanting to take advantage of the more impressive architecture of the main building, the production team decided to use the area between real-life platforms three and four instead of nine and ten which are located in a little annex to the side.

Hungarian Horntail Hot Wings

When Harry faces off against the Norwegian Ridgeback in Harry Potter and the Goblet of Fire, *we get an up-close and personal look at the fire-breathing power of this amazing creature. For filming, its impressive fieriness was achieved with a flamethrower that could shoot fire up to thirty feet! For this dragon-inspired party appetizer, we're achieving it with cayenne and habanero. Add as much or as little spice as you like to control the fierceness of these wings.*

Yield: 24 wings

1 cup flour

1 tablespoon salt

1 tablespoon fresh ground black pepper

24 chicken wings, separated into two pieces

Canola oil, for frying

One 12-ounce bottle homemade or store-bought cayenne hot pepper wing sauce

½ cup (1 stick) butter

2 tablespoons fresh horseradish, minced

1 habanero chile, minced

In a medium bowl, combine flour with salt and pepper.

Dredge chicken wings in flour mixture, and set aside.

Pour about 2 inches of canola into a high-sided cast iron skillet or Dutch oven fitted with a fry thermometer. Slowly bring the oil up to 375°F.

Meanwhile, combine hot pepper sauce, butter, minced horseradish, and minced habanero in a medium saucepan over low heat. Simmer for 5 to 10 minutes.

Fry dredged chicken wings in canola oil in batches for 5 to 7 minutes, or until cooked through (the internal temperature should read 165°F). Remove from oil and place on a paper-towel-lined rack or plate while you cook the remaining wings.

Once wings are cooked, place them in a large bowl that has a cover. Pour hot wing sauce over wings, place cover on bowl, and shake well to coat all sides of the wings.

Serve immediately.

Behind the Magic

Multiple models were created for the Hungarian Horntail during filming, including a forty-foot-long, seven-foot-tall puppet for the scene where the Horntail arrives at Hogwarts in her cage. Since the dragon had to breathe fire, the head of the puppet had to be recast in fiberglass and the snout coated in Nomex—a substance that made it fireproof. The beak was made out of steel, which glowed red when heated by the fire from the flamethrower.

FLYING BROOMSTICK CAKE POPS

*Broomsticks are an important means of magical travel—and fun, as they are used
in the wizarding world's most popular sport, Quidditch. A delectable blend of sweet
and salty, this brownie-based cake pop is sculpted to look just like your favorite
brooms from the films. They will surely sweep your guests right off their feet.*

Yield: 12 to 14 pops

FOR THE BROWNIE CAKE

6 tablespoons (¾ stick) butter

2 ounces unsweetened chocolate,
broken up into small pieces

1 cup sugar

2 eggs

¾ cup flour

FOR THE CAKE POPS

5 ounces caramel bits, melted

1 tablespoon water

15 ounces semisweet chocolate
melting wafers

One 11-ounce bag butterscotch
chips

12 to 14 long pretzel rods

TIP

These can be stored
in an airtight container
separated by parchment
for 3 to 5 days. Or they
can be packaged in
cellophane bags to give
as favors.

TO MAKE THE BROWNIE CAKE

Preheat the oven to 350°F, and line an 8-by-8-inch baking pan with
parchment, allowing it to overhang slightly.

In a large microwave-safe bowl, microwave the butter and chocolate together in 10-second increments, stirring in between bursts.
When the chocolate is completely melted and the mixture is
smooth, add in the sugar, stirring to incorporate. Add the eggs 1 at
a time, mixing thoroughly after each addition. Add the flour, and
stir until totally incorporated.

Pour the batter into the prepared pan, and bake for 25 to 30
minutes or until a cake tester comes out clean or with only a few
crumbs. Allow to cool for 15 minutes, then use parchment to lift
the brownie from the pan. Refrigerate for 30 minutes or overnight.

TO MAKE THE CAKE POPS

In a microwave-safe bowl or measuring cup, microwave the caramel and water together in short bursts, stirring in between, until
completely melted.

In a large bowl, use a wooden spoon to break up the brownie into
an even, coarse-crumb texture. Add the melted caramel, and stir
until well combined. Refrigerate for 30 minutes.

Prepare 2 cookie sheets with baking mats or parchment. Have
your pretzel rods close at hand.

Working with about 3 tablespoons of chilled brownie mixture, use
your hands to form a thick patty out of the crumb mix and place a
pretzel rod about halfway through the center of the top of it. Close
the brownie mixture around the rod and shape the remaining
portion into the "bristle" section of the broom. Gently press the
bottom of the broom onto the cookie sheet creating a flat bottom.
Lay the broom down and repeat with the remaining pretzels and
brownie mixture.

"LOOK AT IT: THE NEW NIMBUS 2000!
IT'S THE FASTEST MODEL YET!"

Young wizard, *Harry Potter and the Sorcerer's Stone*

Freeze the broom pops for 30 minutes.

In a medium microwave-safe bowl, microwave the semisweet chocolate in short bursts. Stir frequently, and be careful not to overheat.

Dip each frozen broom pop into the melted chocolate. Use a spatula to gently coat the entire "bristle" portion. Make sure to get chocolate on the joint between the pretzel and the brownie mixture to seal the cake pop to the pretzel rod. Shake the pop gently over the bowl to remove excess chocolate, and set the flat bottom back on the cookie sheet, so the broom is now standing.

Repeat with the remaining brooms until they are all coated in the dark chocolate. Save any remaining chocolate, and set aside.

In another microwave-safe bowl, microwave the butterscotch chips in short bursts, being careful not to overheat.

Use a pastry brush (silicone works best) to brush the melted butterscotch chips onto the cake portion of each broom pop. Work slowly in long strokes, and let the lines show to create a bristle texture. Repeat with all the broom pops.

If necessary, gently reheat the semisweet chocolate. Fill a pastry bag with the chocolate, snip a small hole in the end, and pipe the broom bands onto each brownie pop. Allow 10 to 15 minutes to set.

Continued on page 108

Making the Flying Broomstick Cake Pops

ʙEHIND
THE ᴍAGIC

As props, the broomsticks in the Harry Potter films had a lot of work to do. To stand up to all of the wear and tear that comes with a prop that is going to be handled, sat on, attached to motion-control bases, the broomsticks had to be thin and "incredibly durable," says propmaker Pierre Bohanna. To keep the brooms lightweight but strong, they were crafted out of aircraft-grade titanium, which was then covered in mahogany wood with birch branches added for the bristle head.

ABOVE: Prop broomsticks created for the Harry Potter films.

Prefect Fizzy Floats

Inspired by the gushing multicolored taps of the Prefects' bathroom in Harry Potter and the Goblet of Fire, *these bubbly colorful drinks are worth spending a couple hours in detention. Make the syrups ahead of time and have them on hand for quick assembly right before your party begins!*

Yield: 12 servings

FOR THE PINEAPPLE SYRUP
1 tablespoon turbinado sugar
½ teaspoon turmeric
1½ cups pineapple juice

FOR THE STRAWBERRY SYRUP
2 cups fresh strawberries, hulled and quartered
1 cup water
1 cup sugar

FOR THE GINGER SYRUP
1 cup water
4 ounces fresh ginger, peeled and sliced thin
1 cup sugar
2 tablespoons butterfly pea flower tea

FOR THE FLOATS
2 tablespoons red, green, or blue syrup (see accompanying recipes), for each serving
1 carton vanilla ice cream
1 liter sparkling water

SPECIAL SUPPLIES
Champagne flutes or Collins glasses

TO MAKE THE PINEAPPLE SYRUP

In a small saucepan over medium-high heat, add the sugar and turmeric. Cook, stirring until the mixture is fragrant and the sugar is just beginning to smoke.

Add the pineapple juice and stir to deglaze the pan. Bring the mixure to a simmer and simmer for about 10 minutes or until the mixture is reduced by a third.

Store syrup in an airtight container in the refrigerator for up to 1 week.

TO MAKE THE STRAWBERRY SYRUP

In a medium saucepan over medium-high heat, add all the ingredients, and bring to a boil. Boil for 2 to 3 minutes.

Turn off heat, and allow syrup to cool 15 to 20 minutes.

Puree the syrup in a blender, and strain through a fine sieve, pressing as much juice from the berries as possible and leaving behind the seeds. Store in an airtight container in the refrigerator for up to 1 week.

Behind the Magic

The set for the Prefects' bathroom features an enormous room-sized tub filled by dozens of taps that dispense streams of steamy red, yellow, and green-colored water. The taps were sand-cast in bronze to ensure durability during filming.

TO MAKE THE GINGER SYRUP

In a small saucepan over medium-high heat, add the water, ginger, and sugar, and bring to a simmer. Simmer, stirring constantly, until all sugar is dissolved.

Remove syrup from heat, and add in butterfly pea flower. Allow to steep 20 to 25 minutes.

Strain syrup in a fine mesh sieve, and store in an airtight container for up to 1 week.

TO ASSEMBLE THE FLOATS

Add 2 tablespoons of the desired syrup to the bottom of a champagne flute or Collins glass.

Using a small scoop (1 to 2 inches), place 2 scoops of ice cream on top of the syrup.

Fill the glass with sparkling water. Serve immediately with long spoons or straws if desired.

HARRY POTTER BINGO

There are two ways to play this fun Harry Potter Bingo game. First is the traditional way, where a caller pulls cards and names the item while players mark off their bingo cards. But an alternate and very fun way to do this during a movie marathon is to give each guest a bingo card and have guests mark their cards when a character, location, or element appears on the screen! Either way, the first player to achieve five in a row in any direction wins a prize of your choosing.

- Harry Potter Bingo card printables ⊙
- White cardstock
- Items for marking cards (pennies, pebbles, etc.)

1. Download our Harry Potter Bingo card printables from our online resources. Print on white cardstock, and cut them out individually.

2. If using the calling cards, print those out and place in a bowl for the caller to pull out for each turn. Once a card has been called, set it aside, and pull a new card from the bowl.

3. The first player to get five consecutive squares in any direction wins.

TIP
Use Bertie Bott's Every Flavor Beans as card markers to add a fun twist.

HARRY POTTER TEMPORARY TATTOOS

Leave your mark with this collection of Harry Potter temporary tattoos. Featuring a range of iconic images including lightning bolts, the Deathly Hallows symbol, and more, there is something for everyone.

- Harry Potter Temporary Tattoos printables ⊙
- Temporary tattoo printable paper
- Scissors

1. Download our pattern for Harry Potter Temporary Tattoos printables from our online resources.

2. Print and cut out designs on temporary tattoo paper.

3. Follow instructions on temporary tattoo paper to apply the tattoos.

4. Set out the cut designs on the coffee table near your TV so guests can have fun applying them during the films!

PREVIOUS PAGE: A box of Bertie Botts' Every Flavour Beans. Packaging designed by graphic artists Miraphora Mina and Eduardo Lima. RIGHT: Ron Weasley attempts to perform a spell on Scabbers on board the Hogwarts Express in a behind-the-scenes shot from *Harry Potter and the Sorcerer's Stone.*

CHOCOLATE FROGS

It wouldn't be a trip aboard the Hogwarts Express without Chocolate Frogs. While we can't promise these will hop away like the frogs in the film, they still make a great favor to send with your guests after the party. A chocolate mold and our printable boxes help make this an easy do-in-advance craft.

- 10 ounces semisweet or milk chocolate melting wafers
- 3-inch chocolate frog molds
- Chocolate Frog Box template ⊙
- Cardstock
- Bone folder or credit card
- Glue

TO MAKE THE CHOCOLATE FROGS

1. Pour about half the chocolate wafers into a microwave-safe bowl, and microwave on half power (or defrost) for 30 seconds. Stir and add the rest of the chocolate. Microwave again, still on half power, for another 30 seconds, and then stir until smooth. If a little more heat is needed to melt the chocolate, microwave again in 15-second bursts, stirring between each burst.

2. Once the chocolate is completely smooth, gently stir for 3 to 5 minutes until it thickens slightly. Pour the chocolate into the frog molds, and tap several times on the counter to help it settle and release air bubbles. Let the molds cool on the counter for 20 minutes, and then refrigerate for 10 to 20 minutes until solid. To remove the frogs, gently flex the mold until each one pops out.

Continued on page 116

TIP

For an extra touch of authenticity, create your own collectible Famous Wizard Card to insert into the lid of your Chocolate Frog box. To do so, cut a pentagon out of construction paper big enough that it won't fall out of the lid, but not so big that it can't be easily taken in and out. Then you can draw and decorate any famous witch or wizard you like!

Making the Chocolate Frog Box

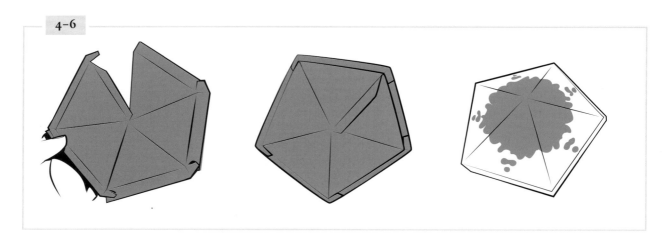

4–6

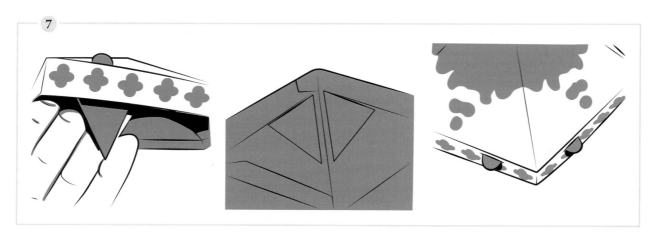

7

8

TO MAKE THE BOX

3. Download the Chocolate Frog Box template from the online resources. Print all components (front and back) on heavy cardstock. Print as many copies as you need for your chocolate frogs.

4. Cut the individual components out along the dotted lines. Use a bone folder or the edge of a credit card to score along the solid lines. Fold the pieces along the score lines to get a crisp fold.

5. On piece A, glue the largest tab to create a pointed lid.

6. Glue all small tabs on piece A to the inside of the box sides to close the sides.

7. Glue pieces B and C flat against the inside of the lids with round tabs sticking through the holes on the lid. This will help the box stay closed later.

8. Glue the supports (pieces D and E) to the inside of the lid, lining up the long sides of the support pieces with the left and right sides of the lid (the top of the lid should be pointing away from you). Set the lid aside to dry.

9. Glue all small tabs of the box bottom (piece F) to bring the sides of the box bottom together, using the dark shaded areas as guides.

10. Glue the top lid to the base, using the shaded areas as guides.

11. Repeat with remaining boxes until all are assembled.

12. Place a Chocolate Frog inside each box, and set them out where your guests can grab one before they go home.

BEHIND THE MAGIC

Unlike the other paintings and photographs in the Harry Potter films, the image of Professor Dumbledore on Harry's first-ever Chocolate Frog card was made from the same foil material used to create a 3D hologram.

The Yule Ball Holiday Celebration

"The Yule Ball has been a tradition of the Triwizard Tournament since its inception."

Professor McGonagall, *Harry Potter and the Goblet of Fire*

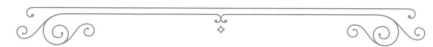

THE YULE BALL
HOLIDAY CELEBRATION

Harry Potter and the Goblet of Fire expands the wizarding world beyond Hogwarts and Britain by introducing the Triwizard Tournament and two new schools of magic, Durmstrang Institute and Beauxbatons Academy of Magic. Designed to be an exercise in international magical cooperation, the tournament instead pits the three schools against one another, except for one special occasion: the Yule Ball. While the holidays at Hogwarts are always a visual feast for moviegoers, the Yule Ball takes it to a new level, transforming the Great Hall into a glittering ice palace. Now you can celebrate the holidays in true wizarding style by hosting your very own celebration inspired by the festive event.

As the Yule Ball is, as Professor McGonagall puts it, "first and foremost a dance," this party is best held in a large, open space with room for a dance floor and multiple small tables. Because the event is nondenominational, the décor focuses on a snowy theme (as the production designers and set decorators did when they planned the real Yule Ball). Craft your own Magical Snowfall backdrop to drape the walls or hang around the dance floor. Paired with traditional elements like silvery-blue table linens and candelabra, this simple craft goes a long way toward turning a room into a magical winter wonderland. The menu suggestions for the party features delights inspired by northern Europe to honor Durmstrang, and some classic French fare to represent Beauxbatons. Of course Hogwarts is also included, with Scotch eggs, fish and chips, and classic mushy peas—a pub favorite!

But the magical cooperation doesn't end there. In addition to the Golden Egg Scavenger Hunt, which is sure to keep your guests on their toes, we've also provided inspiration for creating a Harry Potter Photo Booth, festive signage, and school crest name tags so your guests can choose who they'd most like to represent.

Put on your dress robes; the Yule Ball is about to begin!

EVENT OVERVIEW

INVITATION
- Yule Ball Invitation

DECORATIONS
- Yule Ball Backdrop
- Magical Snowfall

MENU SUGGESTIONS
- Hagrid's Secret Dragon Eggs
- Professor Karkaroff's Caviar-Topped Deviled Eggs
- Madame Maxime's Giant Potato Gratin
- Black Lake Fish & Chips
- The Hog's Head Mushy Peas
- Yule Ball Cultural Celebration Cakes
- The Four Champions' Spiced Cider

ACTIVITIES
- The Golden Egg Scavenger Hunt
- Harry Potter Photo Booth Props
- School Crest Name Tags
- *Daily Prophet* Wizard Crackers

FAVORS
- Triwizard Paper Ornaments

Yule Ball Invitation

Based on the real Yule Ball program created for the film by graphic artists Miraphora Mina and Eduardo Lima, these miniature ice palace invitations are sure to thrill your guests and strike the perfect tone for your party. The gatefold invitation card opens to reveal the party details. While an electric cutting machine makes it easier to create this, we have included a PDF version, which you may cut out with scissors. Icy blue or pearlized envelopes would be a beautiful complement to this sparkling invitation.

- Yule Ball Invitation printable ⊙
- Electric cutting machine such as a Cricut or scissors
- White, icy blue, and glitter cardstock
- Bone folder
- Double-sided tape or glue
- A7 envelopes

1. Download our Yule Ball Invitation printable from our online resources.

2. If using an electric cutting machine like a Cricut, upload the SVG files to your design software, and fill in the details for your party. Print, then cut the invitation (the piece with the party details) on the white cardstock. Cut out a backing card for the invitation in icy blue cardstock (or complementary color of your choice). Finally, cut out the gatefold castle shape on the glitter or white cardstock according to your machine's directions.

3. If using the PDF version, open the invitation in Adobe Reader. Fill in the details for your party in the editable fields. Print and cut out invitation on white cardstock. Cut out a backing card for the invitation in a contrasting cardstock (we used icy blue). Finally cut out the gatefold castle design, and use this as a pattern to cut your glitter cardstock.

4. Score the cardstock using a bone folder or credit card, and fold each side of the gatefold so that it opens and closes easily.

5. Attach white invitation to the contrasting backing card with double-sided tape or glue, allowing at least a quarter inch if not more around each edge.

Behind the Magic

The Yule Ball program, created by Miraphora Mina and Eduardo Lima, featured cutout letters, pop-out snowflakes, and an architectural outline to echo the elaborate ice sculptures in the Great Hall. The graphics department also created a poster and a dance card for the special event.

You are cordially invited to join us for the

Yule Ball

Saturday, December 1st
Seven o'clock in the evening
Professor Albus Dumbledore
Hogwarts School of Witchcraft & Wizardry
R.S.V.P.
Dumbledore@Hogwarts.com
BLACK TIE OPTIONAL

6. Attach the invite with backing card to the center of the castle gatefold with double-sided tape or glue. Make sure the gatefold opens and closes easily with the card placement.

7. Place inside envelopes.

8. Stamp your envelopes, address them, and put them in the post!

YULE BALL BACKDROP

Welcome your guests to the Yule Ball with this oversize replica of the Yule Ball invitation! This sign backdrop can be used in multiple places throughout your party, including at the welcome table where guests select their name tags, as a backdrop for the buffet table, or even incorporated into your photo booth backdrop! The possibilities are endless. We recommend printing this through your local print shop on poster paper and then attaching it to poster board for strength and durability.

- Yule Ball Sign backdrop template ⬇
- Two 22-by-28-inch poster boards
- Scissors
- Double-sided tape or glue

1. Download our Yule Ball Sign backdrop template from our online resources. This backdrop is sized to print on two 24-by-36-inch posters. We recommend printing these through your favorite local print shop.

2. Once printed, cut out details of center castle section and the two side sections.

3. Attach each section to poster board with glue or double-sided tape. You will need one whole poster board for the center section. The side sections should fit side by side on the other.

4. Cut out all sections of the sign.

5. Attach one side section to each side of the center section by gluing or taping the tabs on the sides to the back of the center section.

6. Display!

Styling Magic!

Set decorator Stephenie McMillan used drapery to transform the Great Hall into a silvery ice palace for the Yule Ball. The team located and bought massive amounts of fireproof silver Lurex fabric, and they fastened it to the walls, wrapped it around the trusses, draped it from the windows, and used it to cover the tables. What wasn't swathed in fabric was still silver, including the Christmas trees that bordered the room and the instruments for the twenty-four-piece orchestra. "It just sort of gathered momentum," confesses McMillan. The icy theme carried throughout, from the blue-lit ice in the flambeau bowls to the icicle-encrusted ceiling.

You don't need to be a professional set decorator to transform your space into an elegant homage to the Yule Ball. However, if you have a little budget to splurge, you can take your party to the next level by renting a bit of party décor, including round tables, linens, and specialty chairs. For reference, a five-foot-round table can seat eight to ten adults. There are endless options for linens; look for pale blues, shimmering whites, and luxe silvers to mimic the colors of the ball in the film. A large branch or small tree spray-painted white or silver makes for a dramatic centerpiece and a great place to hang your Triwizard Ornaments. Additional small details like faux florals in silver and blue and snow-drop-like crystals complete the effect of turning your large entertaining space into an icy winter wonderland.

ABOVE: A set photo of the Great Hall decorated for the Yule Ball in *Harry Potter and the Goblet of Fire*.

MAGICAL SNOWFALL

The teachers at Hogwarts transform the Great Hall into a magical snow-covered ice palace through clever spellcraft. Thanks to this simple craft you can create a backdrop that achieves the same elegant, snowy effect. While this project is simple to do, you may want to start several weeks in advance to give yourself time to make as many hanging strips as you desire. You could use this to create a dramatic entrance to your party, to anchor your dance floor space, or to decorate any other place you want a dramatic backdrop.

- Magical Snowfall template ⬇
- White copy paper
- Pencil
- Scissors
- Double-sided tape
- Floral-safe Glitter spray
- White crochet thread, classic size #10
- Masking tape
- Needle
- White ribbon
- Command-strip hooks

1. Download our Magical Snowfall template from our online resources.

2. Cut out the template, and use it as a pattern.

3. Fold a piece of copy paper in half. Place the half-circle pattern against the folded edge of the paper. Trace the semicircle pattern with a pencil.

4. Cut along the line. When you unfold the paper you now have a complete circle.

5. Cut the circle along the fold line so that you now have two half-circles.

6. Repeat for as many cones as you wish to use.

7. Curl one half-circle, and place a piece of double-sided tape on one edge to attach it to itself once it's in a cone shape. Try to make the opening on the small end as tight as possible while still leaving enough room for a needle to pass through.

8. Cut your crochet thread to the desired finished length of your drape. Repeat for as many lengths as you need for your party space.

9. Tear a piece of masking tape, and wrap it at the base of your piece of crochet thread. This will act as a stop to keep your cone from sliding off. You can try tying a knot in the thread, but we found a wider barrier like masking tape makes this process much simpler.

TIP

Glitter spray is available at craft stores and even the paint aisles of many home improvement stores, or online.

10. Thread a needle on your other end of the crochet thread, and thread your needle through the small end of your cone. Repeat with as many cones as you desire to have on each thread.

11. Once your cones are threaded, go ahead and space them evenly along the string. Attach wrapped masking tape at each point where you want the cones to stop.

12. Working in a well-ventilated area, spray your cones with a healthy coat of glitter spray to make them twinkle and shine. Set aside until completely dry, according to the directions on the can.

13. Cut a length of ribbon as wide as you need for where you plan to hang this drape.

14. Tie the top of the string that has been strung with cones to the ribbon. Use command strip hooks to hang.

TIP

To store, keep the cones on the string, and simply stack them upside down, careful not to tangle your thread. This will keep them ready and waiting for you to simply hang on party day!

HAGRID'S SECRET DRAGON EGGS

The Scotch egg is a British classic. Here we are giving it a Potter spin inspired by Hagrid's love of dragons and the iconic scene from Harry Potter and the Sorcerer's Stone *when he hatches a secret dragon egg in his hut. Hard-boiled eggs take a dramatically delicious turn with the addition of savory sausage and a crispy coating styled to look like the shiny scales of different breeds. Keep a bottle of hot sauce handy, as it can help kick up the heat for those looking to add a little fire to their serving.*

YIELD: 6 EGGS

12 ounces bulk sausage

6 hard-boiled eggs, peeled and chilled

About 6 ounces red or golden beet chips

About 6 ounces, purple potato chips

About 4 ounces, snap pea crisps

¼ cup tapioca flour

1 egg, beaten

About 2 quarts of oil

Mustard, for dipping

TIP
Wetting your hands with cold water will keep the sausage from sticking to you while you are wrapping the eggs.

Have a large plate standing by. Divide the sausage equally into six patties. Wrap each egg in a sausage patty, smoothing and shaping the sausage to cover the entire egg. Set on the plate. Repeat with all the eggs, then refrigerate while prepping the other ingredients.

In the bowl of a food processer, pulverize each type of chip separately until it is a fine crumb. You should have about a three-quarter cup of each coating or a little over 2 cups total. Split each coating in half, and place them in separate shallow bowls. You should now have six total bowls, two of each kind, if you are doing all three colors.

Place the tapioca flour and beaten egg in separate shallow bowls to set up your dredging station. Set up one bowl of each coating next to the dredging station, and one bowl of each coating in a separate location near the deep-fryer. It is very important to separate the bowls of coating at this stage to prevent cross-contamination.

Remove the eggs from the refrigerator.

Using either a deep fryer or a Dutch oven fitted with a fry thermometer, bring the oil up to 365°F.

Dip each egg first into the tapioca flour, then into the egg, then into the desired coating.

Fry one or two eggs at a time for 6 minutes each. Using tongs, remove from the fryer and immediately recoat in the matching coating using the fresh, uncontaminated bowl next to your deep fryer. Repeat until all the eggs are fried.

Let the eggs rest for 5 to 10 minutes, and then serve warm or refrigerate and serve cold with good quality mustard.

Professor Karkaroff's Caviar-Topped Deviled Eggs

There's no doubt that Professor Karkaroff enjoys the finer things in life, and these decadent deviled eggs are no exception. Topped with caviar as a nod to the Durmstrang Institute's purported Northern European background and location and Karkaroff's taste for high-end living, the filling also includes spicy German mustard to give these eggs a little kick.

Yield: 12 deviled eggs

6 eggs in shell
Water, for boiling eggs
¼ cup mayonnaise
2 tablespoons Bavarian mustard or spicy mustard of your choice
Salt and fresh ground black pepper
Smoked paprika, for garnish
Caviar or Cavi-art, for garnish

Place eggs in a saucepan, and add water to cover eggs. Heat to a boil.

Boil for 2 minutes and turn off heat. Cover pan and allow eggs to sit for approximately 10 minutes.

Remove eggs from water and place them in an ice bath to cool completely.

Once eggs have cooled, peel shells.

Slice eggs in half lengthwise. Place hard yolks in a medium bowl, and set hollowed-out eggs aside.

Combine yolks with mayonnaise, mustard, salt and pepper to taste. Blend until creamy.

Fill hollowed eggs with yolk mixture.

Garnish with paprika and Cavi-art. Serve immediately.

Madame Maxime's Giant Potato Gratin

First introduced in Harry Potter and the Goblet of Fire, *Beauxbatons Academy of Magic is a French school of magic presided over by Madame Maxime, a charismatic, richly dressed half-giantess who, in the words of the actress Frances de la Tour who played her, "is in serious denial about being big." In honor of Madame Maxime and her impressive stature, this recipe takes a traditional French classic and adapts it for the buffet table with individual cheesy potato stacks that are easy for people to serve themselves.*

Yield: 12 stacks, serves 6 to 8

2 pounds large russet potatoes
1 cup grated Parmesan
2 cups shredded fontina
2 cups half-and-half
½ teaspoon thyme
½ teaspoon rosemary
1 teaspoon parsley flakes
1 teaspoon kosher salt
4 tablespoons butter, softened
Fresh parsley for garnish, optional

Preheat the oven to 450°F.

Cut the potatoes lengthwise using a mandoline or a very sharp chef's knife, creating long oval slices.

In a large bowl, mix the cheeses together, and set aside.

In a medium saucepan over medium heat, combine the half-and-half with the spices and salt. Bring to a simmer and cook for 1 to 2 minutes. Remove from the heat, and set aside.

Grease the bottom and sides of an 11-by-17-inch rimmed baking sheet with butter. Place slices of potato on the baking sheet, touching but not overlapping. Start to build stacks of potatoes by sprinkling a bit of cheese mixture on each potato and placing another slice on top. Continue until the stacks are 3 to 4 slices high, sprinkling a bit of cheese on each layer. Reserve some cheese for the final baking step.

Gently pour the half-and-half mixture over the potatoes and seal the whole baking sheet with foil.

Bake for 20 to 30 minutes until the potatoes are fork tender. Remove the foil, sprinkle the remaining cheese on each stack, and bake another 15 to 20 minutes or until golden brown.

Garnish with fresh parsley, if using.

Black Lake Fish & Chips

For the second task in the Triwizard Tournament, the champions must retrieve a "treasure of sorts" from the murky depths of Hogwarts's famous Black Lake. Inspired by the task's watery setting, this recipe offers a fresh take on a British classic by using blue corn chips to darken the batter, thus turning ordinary fish and chips into a feast worthy of the Black Lake.

Yield: 6 servings

FOR THE CHIPS

2 tablespoons kosher salt, plus more for sprinkling (optional)

4 cups water

2 pounds russet or purple potatoes, washed and scrubbed

About 2 quarts frying oil such as canola oil or safflower oil

FOR THE FISH

2 pounds skinless, boneless cod or tilapia

About 2 quarts frying oil

¼ cup mayonnaise

½ cup milk

Juice of 1 lemon

1 cup flour

2 cups crushed blue corn chips, about 1 bag

½ teaspoon cayenne

½ teaspoon kosher salt

Salt, for sprinkling (optional)

TO MAKE THE GLAZE

In a large bowl, dissolve the salt into the water.

Cut the unpeeled potatoes into sticks about a quarter-inch thick. Place all the potatoes in the salted water, and let soak for 30 minutes to 1 hour. Drain the water, and place the potatoes on paper towels to dry.

In a large Dutch oven or deep fryer, over medium-high heat, start to bring the oil up to 365°F. For best results, use a fry thermometer to monitor the oil temperature.

When the oil is ready, fry the potatoes in small batches until very golden brown. Drain on a wire rack, and sprinkle with more salt if desired.

Continued on page 134

RIGHT: Students gather at the Black Lake to watch the second task in *Harry Potter and the Goblet of Fire.*

TO MAKE THE FISH

Cut the fish into pieces about 2 inches by 5 inches, and about an inch thick.

In a large Dutch oven or deep fryer, over medium-high heat, start to bring the oil up to 365°F. For best results, use a fry thermometer to monitor the oil temperature.

While the oil is heating, mix the mayonnaise, milk, and lemon juice together in a large shallow dish and have standing by. Mix the salt and cayenne into the flour. Pour the flour and crushed chips into two separate shallow dishes, creating the dredging station.

When the oil is ready, coat each piece of fish first in the flour, then in the milk mixture, then in the crushed chips.

Working with two or three pieces at a time, fry the fish in the oil for 4 to 5 minutes until it is flaky and cooked through.

Place on a wire rack to drain. Sprinkle with salt if desired.

BEHIND THE MAGIC

The underwater scenes were filmed on a set where a huge tank was built measuring 60 feet on a side and 20 feet deep, and holding half a million gallons of water. To allow the director and cameraman to follow the action, there was a window in one side of the tank with 3-inch-thick glass. To avoid the actors having to dive and then surface for air over and over again, the crew built a special habitat inside the tank, which the actors could access through an air lock, so they could rest and catch their breath between takes.

THE HOG'S HEAD MUSHY PEAS

Mushy peas are a classic British recipe no self-respecting pub would forget—even one with a slightly dubious reputation like the Hog's Head. We imagine this comforting classic as a menu staple at Aberforth Dumbledore's pub, something Mundungus Fletcher would enjoy during his frequent visits. The perfect accompaniment to the Black Lake Fish & Chips, serve these peas in a rustic bowl with a big spoon for self-serving at your next buffet.

YIELD: 4 SERVINGS

1 green onion, sliced
2 tablespoons extra-virgin olive oil
2 cups shelled fresh peas (or frozen)
Water
½ lemon, juiced
6 fresh mint leaves, torn
Salt and fresh ground black pepper

In a medium pan over medium heat, sauté onion in olive oil for about a minute to soften.

Add peas to the pan along with enough water to just barely cover them. Cook over high heat for approximately 2 minutes if using fresh peas and approximately 4 minutes if using frozen.

Add in lemon juice and mint leaves, and cook for 2 more minutes.

Season with salt and pepper to taste, and serve immediately.

ABOVE: Concept art of the Hog's Head Pub in Hogsmeade by Andrew Williamson for *Harry Potter and the Half-Blood Prince.*

Yule Ball Cultural Celebration Cakes

Harry Potter and the Goblet of Fire *introduces two new wizarding schools: from the north, Durmstrang Institute, led by the sinister Professor Karkaroff, and from France, Beauxbatons Academy, led by the towering, fashionable Madame Maxime. Here we celebrate the unique flavors of the regions of the three schools from the tournament: a French Vanilla cake for Beauxbatons, a Black Forest–inspired cake for Durmstrang, and a Gingerbread cake for Hogwarts. We've also created a downloadable stencil for you to customize the tops of your cakes. You can find this in our online resources section.*

YIELD: 8 TO 10 SERVINGS
PER CAKE

SPECIAL SUPPLIES
• Triwizard Tournament 3 Schools Cake Stencil ⬇

FOR THE HOGWARTS CAKE
(GINGERBREAD)

½ cup (1 stick) unsalted butter, softened, plus more for pan

2¼ cups all-purpose flour, plus more for pan

½ cup packed dark brown sugar

1 large egg, at room temperature

1 cup molasses

1 teaspoon vanilla extract

1¼ teaspoons baking soda

1½ teaspoons ground ginger

1½ teaspoons ground cinnamon

½ teaspoon ground cloves

½ teaspoon salt

¾ cup hot water

Powdered sugar, for dusting

FOR THE BEAUXBATONS CAKE
(FRENCH VANILLA)

½ cup (1 stick) unsalted butter, softened, plus more for pan

1½ cups cake flour, plus more for pan

¼ teaspoon salt

½ teaspoon baking powder

¼ teaspoon baking soda

⅓ cup half-an-half or heavy cream

¼ cup sour cream, at room temperature

¾ cup granulated sugar

2 large whole eggs plus 1 egg white, at room temperature

1 tablespoon vanilla extract

Powdered sugar, for dusting

FOR THE DURMSTRANG CAKE
(BLACK FOREST)

FOR THE CHERRY LIQUEUR SYRUP

¼ cup granulated sugar

¼ cup water

3 tablespoons cherry liqueur or kirsch

1 cup cherries, fresh or maraschino, pitted and chopped

FOR THE CAKE

⅓ cup cocoa powder, plus more for pan

1 cup cake flour

1 teaspoon baking soda

½ teaspoon baking powder

1 cup granulated sugar

½ teaspoon salt

1 large egg

1 teaspoon vanilla extract

¼ cup vegetable oil

¼ cup half-and-half

¼ cup sour cream

Powdered sugar, for dusting

TO MAKE THE HOGWARTS CAKE

Preheat the oven to 350°F. Grease and flour an 8-inch cake pan. Set aside.

In the bowl of a stand mixer fitted with a paddle attachment, cream the brown sugar and butter on medium speed. Scrape down the sides, and add the egg, molasses, and vanilla. Mix everything together, scraping down the sides as needed, until combined. Set aside.

In a separate bowl, sift together the flour, baking soda, ginger, cinnamon, cloves, and salt. Fold the dry ingredients into the creamed butter mixture. Gently stir in the hot water, and pour into the prepared pan.

Bake 1 hour or until a toothpick inserted in the center comes out clean. Allow to cool in pan before serving.

Download the Triwizard Tournament 3 Schools Cake Stencils from our online resources, and print on printer paper. Cut along the lines to create the stencils.

Place "H" stencil on top of the cake and dust with powdered sugar. Remove the stencil and serve with the two other cakes, if desired.

TO MAKE THE BEAUXBATONS CAKE

Preheat the oven to 350°F. Line the bottom of an 8-inch cake pan with parchment paper. Butter the parchment, and dust the pans with flour, tapping out the excess. Set aside.

In a medium bowl, sift together the flour, salt, baking powder, and baking soda. Set aside.

Stir half-and-half and sour cream together in a jar or measuring cup, and set aside.

In the bowl of a stand mixer fitted with a paddle attachment, cream the butter and sugar on medium speed until light and fluffy. Reduce the speed, and add the eggs one at a time. Pause to scrape down the sides of the bowl as needed. Add the vanilla, and mix to combine. Slowly add the flour mixture a little at a time. Add some of the half-and-half mixture between the flour additions to help it combine. End with the flour mixture, and blend until smooth.

Pour the batter into the prepared pan, and bake for approximately 30 minutes or until a toothpick inserted in the center comes out clean. Cool in pan for 10 minutes, and then turn out onto a rack to cool completely.

Download the Triwizard Tournament 3 Schools Cake Stencils from our online resources, and print on printer paper. Cut along the lines to create the stencils.

Place "B" stencil on top of the cake and dust with powdered sugar. Remove the stencil, and serve with the other two cakes, if desired.

TO MAKE THE DURMSTRANG CAKE

Begin preparing the cherry syrup by bringing the sugar and water to a boil in a small saucepan over medium-high heat, stirring frequently until the sugar dissolves. Remove from heat, and allow to cool.

Once cool, add in cherry liqueur and cherries, and stir to combine.

Preheat the oven to 350°F. Line the bottom of an 8-inch cake pan with parchment paper. Butter the parchment, and dust the pans with cocoa powder, tapping out the excess. Set aside.

In a large bowl, sift together the flour, cocoa powder, baking soda, and baking powder. Stir in the sugar and salt. Add in the egg, vanilla, oil, half-and-half, and sour cream, and mix to combine. Add in the syrup and the chopped cherries, and mix until the batter is well combined and the cherries are evenly distributed throughout. Pour into the prepared pan.

Bake for 40 minutes or until a toothpick comes out mostly clean. Cool 10 minutes in the pan, then turn out onto a wire rack to cool completely.

Download the Triwizard Tournament 3 Schools Cake Stencils from our online resources, and print on printer paper. Cut along the lines to create the stencils.

Place "D" stencil on top of the cake, and dust with powdered sugar. Remove the stencil, and serve with the other two cakes, if desired.

ABOVE: Stanislav Yanevski, Clémence Posey, and Robert Pattison as Viktor Krum, Fleur Delacour, and Cedric Diggory in a publicity shot for *Harry Potter and the Goblet of Fire.*

THE FOUR CHAMPIONS' SPICED CIDER

The Yule Ball as seen in Harry Potter and the Goblet of Fire *gave us a chance to view Hogwarts in all its Christmas finery. The ball opens with a special dance by the three (or four) Triwizard Champions and their partners. In the film, these champions are Viktor Krum (Durmstrang), Fleur Delacour (Beauxbatons), Cedric Diggory (Hogwarts), and Harry Potter (also Hogwarts). Named in their honor, this special spiced cider is the perfect beverage for the Yule Ball or any other festive, wintry event.*

YIELD: 15 TO 16 SERVINGS

1 gallon apple juice
1 orange, juiced
1 tablespoon ground cinnamon
1 tablespoon allspice
1 tablespoon grated nutmeg (from a whole nutmeg)
1 tablespoon whole cloves
Cinnamon sticks, for garnish

Note: You can easily double this recipe if you are having a larger gathering.

Heat apple juice, orange juice, and all spices in a large pot over medium heat.

Simmer for 15 to 20 minutes until heated through and spices have begun to permeate the cider.

Transfer to a large serving bowl with a ladle. Serve immediately with cinnamon sticks on the side to use as garnish.

ABOVE: The four champions are interviewed by Rita Skeeter, played by Miranda Richardson, in *Harry Potter and the Goblet of Fire.*

THE GOLDEN EGG SCAVENGER HUNT

What's a Yule Ball without a Triwizard challenge? Inspired by the famous Golden Egg from the first task of the Triwizard Tournament, this fun scavenger hunt can be structured several ways, so choose an option that best suits your guest count and your space. Prior to the party, hide several golden eggs around the room. The number of eggs you hide should depend on your guest count. A smaller gathering may include five to eight eggs, but if you are having a large party you may want to hide as many as twenty. We have created game cards you can display at each guest table, explaining the rules of the game and giving you an opportunity to set a time limit on the activity. When the time is up, whoever has the most eggs wins!

- Golden Egg Scavenger Hunt printable ⬇
- Cardstock
- Scissors
- Gold-foil-wrapped candy eggs or gold plastic eggs

1. Download our Golden Egg Scavenger Hunt printable from our online resources.

2. Print on cardstock and cut out cards.

3. Hide golden eggs around party space. Set out a couple in obvious places to encourage participation, but don't be afraid to get creative and consider spots including an ice bucket, a floral centerpiece, the branches of a holiday tree, or even behind the pillows on a couch.

4. Have guests hunt for eggs, and whomever finds the most eggs wins the challenge!

BEHIND THE MAGIC

Inspired in part by Russian Fabergé eggs, the Golden Egg seen in the films was gold-plated and completely waterproof. It weighed ten pounds, which meant actor Daniel Radcliffe had to wear an invisible plastic clip around one hand that connected to a clip on the egg when filming the underwater parts of the bathroom scene, otherwise the egg would tip over and sink as soon as he took one hand off!

HARRY POTTER PHOTO BOOTH PROPS

No special event is complete without a photo booth, whether you rent a professional setup or make your own with a Polaroid-style instant camera. These Harry Potter–themed photo booth props will help guests loosen up and take lots of photos they will cherish for years to come. Create a fun backdrop for your photos—hang several strands of your Magical Snowfall (page 126) or incorporate the Yule Ball Backdrop (page 124).

• Harry Potter Photo Booth Props printables ⊙
• Cardstock
• Scissors
• Dowels
• Silver spray paint
• Tape or glue

1. Download our Photo Booth Props printables from our online resources.

2. Print on cardstock, and cut out designs.

3. In a well-ventilated area, spray your dowels with silver spray paint. Let dry over night.

4. Attach props to dowels with tape or glue.

5. Set them up inside or next to your photo booth so guests can enjoy the magic!

Party Magic!

How do you teach dozens of young actors to waltz in time for the big ball scene? A month of dance lessons in advance—unless, of course, you're Daniel Radcliffe. Radcliffe was so busy filming other scenes he had only four days to learn the Champion's dance before it was shot. After the waltzing, the students let their hair down as a wizarding rock band took the stage. Propmaker Pierre Bohanna crafted the instruments for the band, including a set of twelve-foot-high bagpipes, a fretless bass, a three-necked guitar, and enormous transparent cymbals.

Whether you've hired a professional band like the one that plays at the real Yule Ball or simply cued up a couple great playlists on your iPod, one thing that can really kill a party is an empty dance floor. To avoid this awkward scene, here are a couple tips.

1. In advance of the party, recruit a couple of reliable friends to get right out on the dance floor when the music begins. And you as party host need to join in from the beginning. Most people don't want to be first, so by having a few friends primed and ready to get the dance party started, others will quickly want to join in.

2. Make sure to pack your playlist early with strong, toe-tapping (or wand-tapping) tunes that are irresistible and impossible to sit still while listening to!

ABOVE: Hermione and Viktor Krum dancing at the Yule Ball in *Harry Potter and the Goblet of Fire*.

SCHOOL CREST NAME TAGS

The Triwizard Tournament is a magical competition between three wizarding schools: Hogwarts, Durmstrang, and Beauxbatons. With these School Crest Name Tags, every guest at your Yule Ball party can select their preferred school and proudly wear their new school crest! To further promote magical cooperation, these crests also double as name tags, which will help your guests get to know one another as they mingle.

SUPPLIES
- School Crest Name Tags printables ⊙
- White cardstock
- Gold or silver pens
- Double-sided tape or pins

1. Download our School Crest Name Tags printables from our online resources.

2. If you know in advance the school assignments and guest names, you may open the name tag file in Adobe Reader and fill in the details for your party in the editable fields. Otherwise, leave these blank and allow guests to choose their school and write in their name upon arrival. Tip: A sparkly silver or gold pen will make these handwritten tags look more festive.

3. Print each name tag sheet on white cardstock and cut them out individually.

4. Have straight pins or double-sided tape on hand to attach the tags to your guests.

Daily Prophet Wizard Crackers

Christmas crackers are a treasured holiday tradition in Britain, even for wizards, as we saw when the Weasleys celebrated the holidays at 12 Grimmauld Place in Harry Potter and the Order of the Phoenix. Make your own wizard-worthy crackers with our printable template and easy instructions. Placing these at your dining tables will help add holiday cheer to your place settings. Alternatively, you could have these in a basket at the entrance for guests to crack into at the onset of the party.

SUPPLIES

- *Daily Prophet* Wizard Cracker Wrappers template ⬇
- 8½-by-11-inch printer paper
- Wizard Cracker House Crests template ⬇
- Electric cutting machine such as a Cricut or scissors
- Gold vinyl
- Transfer paper
- Glue stick
- Snaps
- 4½-inch paper rolls or tubes
- Prizes (chocolate frogs, Bertie Bott's Every Flavour Beans, or something else off the trolley cart)
- Hot glue
- Gold glitter ribbon
- Jute twine

TIP

Snaps to make your crackers pop are available online at sites like Etsy or Amazon.

1. Download the *Daily Prophet* Wizard Cracker Wrappers template from our online resources. Print on regular printer paper.

2. Download the Wizard Cracker House Crests template from our online resources. If you are using a cutting machine, upload the SVG version to your design software, and cut out the crests from gold vinyl according to machine and material directions. If you are hand-cutting the design, print the PDF version, and cut it out, then use the cutout as your template to cut the final design out of vinyl.

3. Weed the excess vinyl from the house crests, and place transfer paper over the image. Use your hand or a credit card to firmly press the transfer paper to your design to ensure it's sticking well, then gently peel the paper away from the original vinyl backing so the image

RON WEASLEY: "YOU'RE FRATERNIZING WITH THE ENEMY!"

HERMIONE GRANGER: "THE ENEMY? WHO WAS IT
WANTING HIS AUTOGRAPH?"

Harry Potter and the Goblet of Fire

of the house crest adheres to the transfer paper. Apply the cut vinyl design to the center of a *Daily Prophet* page, then remove the transfer paper.

4. Flip the wrapper over so the nonprinted side is showing. Use a glue stick along the length of the wrapper, close to one edge. (You only need a line of glue as long as the snap.) Gently press the snap into the glue.

5. Fill your paper tube with the prizes.

6. Roll the paper (with the snap on the inside) around the tube, and secure with a glue stick.

7. Use a hot-glue gun to attach the glitter ribbon to the outside edge of each side of the wrapper.

8. Using jute twine, tie off each end of the paper at about where the tube ends and the paper continues. Tie the twine in a bow for a festive touch.

9. Repeat as needed to make as many crackers as you want.

10. To activate the cracker, have two people pull on the ends of the cracker. It will break at one of the ends, and whoever gets the larger end gets the prize inside!

ABOVE: Harry and Ron sit on the sidelines of the Yule Ball with their dates Parvati and Padma Patil in *Harry Potter and the Goblet of Fire*.

TRIWIZARD PAPER ORNAMENTS

At the end of Harry Potter and the Goblet of Fire, *Harry watches the students from the three competing schools mingling together, exchanging hugs and handshakes, swapping addresses, and saying goodbye—proving that the Triwizard Tournament did in fact bring them all together. These Triwizard Paper Ornaments, featuring imagery from the famous tournament, are the perfect favor to mark another occasion that brings people together. We recommend making them well in advance to help make your last-minute details easier to manage. Consider displaying them en masse on a silver or white holiday tree for a stunning and festive Yule Ball look. Guests can choose their own to take home as special keepsake to treasure forever.*

SUPPLIES

- Triwizard Paper Ornaments templates
- Electric cutting machine such as a Cricut or scissors
- White cardstock
- Bone folder or tool to help with folding
- Double-sided tape or glue
- Ribbon

1. Download our Triwizard Paper Ornaments templates from our online resources.

2. If using an electric cutting machine, upload the SVG files to your design software. Use the Print and Cut feature to make these according to your machine's directions. You will need three panels per ornament.

3. If using the PDF version, open the printables in Adobe Reader. Print the ornament pieces—you will need three panels per ornament. Cut out the ornament shapes with scissors.

4. Once you have three panels per design, fold each panel in half lengthwise. Use a bone folder or other folding tool to help ensure you have a crisp fold. With all three panels folded in half, begin attaching a half-fold of one panel to the half-fold of the next panel with double-sided tape or glue.

5. Before you seal the last folds to each other, place a piece of looped ribbon inside the ornament, leaving enough of a loop outside for hanging. Attach the ribbon to the inside with tape, and then seal the final folds together.

6. Repeat with remaining ornaments, and display on a tree, garland, centerpiece, or other decorative spot where guests can choose one to take home.

A Wizarding Wedding Reception

" YOUNG LOVE! HOW . . . STIRRING."

Rita Skeeter, *Harry Potter and the Goblet of Fire*

Wish us a
year to last
FOREVER
If you would like for us to
share a wedded kiss
Ring the
Golden Smith
for lifelong
bliss!

MAGNIFICENT
MARMALADE

MAGNIFICENT
MARMALADE

MAGNIFICENT
MARMALADE

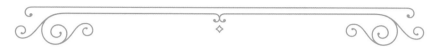

A Wizarding Wedding Reception

The Harry Potter films are filled with acts of love. They're woven into the fabric of the story; we see it in Lily's love for her son, Snape's love for Lily, and most critically, Harry's love for his friends and his willingness to sacrifice himself for them. It's no surprise that love is the strongest magic of all, which is why we've chosen "Powerful Love Creates Powerful Magic" as the theme for this wedding reception. A simple yet elegant affair, this reception is designed to be held in your own home or backyard. While we've planned for a small, intimate gathering, this party can easily be scaled up if you have more guests. Teeming with many beloved elements from all eight films, this party will help you set the stage to honor a love that will last for "always."

A wedding feast is a unique meal, and it's particularly meaningful as this is the first opportunity a married couple has to host their friends and family. Our menu suggestions pull inspiration from a variety of places in the films to offer a slightly upscale dining experience that is still friendly to home cooks everywhere. Dishes include two main dishes to suit different dietary preferences, and for a sweet showstopper centerpiece, the Patronus Pull Charm Cake, which can be reserved for the wedding party or shared with guests, as you prefer.

In terms of crafts and décor, we provide templates and instructions for several simple crafts to bring your event to life with great wizarding style. Welcome your guests to the party with an enchanting message from the Mirror of Erised. Set up an Owl Post Gift Station for gifts and cards. Personalize your dishware with a Potter-inspired message based on the party theme. There are also a variety of wizard-themed activities to keep guests entertained throughout the event, including Quidditch Bean Bag Toss and Golden Snitch–inspired Kissing Bells.

Steeped in the magic and love of the Harry Potter films, this reception is the perfect way to start your life with your chosen one.

EVENT OVERVIEW

INVITATION
- Prophecy Wedding Invitation

DECORATIONS
- Flying Key Place Cards
- "Powerful Love Creates Powerful Magic" Charger Plates & Glasses
- Golden Snitch Kissing Bells
- Deathly Hallows Wreath
- Mirror of Erised Welcome Message
- Owl Post Gift Station

MENU SUGGESTIONS
- Triwizard Charcuterie Board
- Portraits of Scabbers Cheeseboard
- Bezoar Bruschetta
- Professor Sprout's Signature Salad
- Sorcerer's Stone Alchemical Bacon-Wrapped Potatoes
- Sign of the Hallows Rosemary Shrimp Skewers
- Professor Lockhart's Five-Time Award-Winning Most Charming Lasagna Rolls
- Letter from Hogwarts Jam Pastries
- Three Broomsticks Butterscotch Pudding
- Patronus Charm Pull Cake

ACTIVITY
- Quidditch Bean Bag Toss

FAVORS
- Mrs. Weasley's Homemade Jam Jars With Labels

PROPHECY WEDDING INVITATION

Send your guests a prophecy of true love with this special wedding invitation, inspired by the famous prophecy from Harry Potter and the Order of the Phoenix. *Featuring an adorable foldable box with a globe encasing a silhouette of the happy couple in the center, this invitation makes a big impact yet is surprisingly easy to make. We predict your guests will love it!*

- Prophecy Wedding Invitation template ⬇
- Scissors
- Two sheets of 12-by-12-inch square cardstock in coordinating but different colors (box bottom)
- Ruler
- Pencil
- Double-sided tape or glue
- One sheet of 8½-by-11-inch cardstock in coordinating color (for box top)
- Bone folder or credit card
- One sheet of 8½-by-11-inch white cardstock (invitation cards)
- Electric cutting machine (Cricut)
- Cardstock in color of your choice (wizard couple silhouette)
- 4-inch plastic fish bowl

Note: The above supplies create one invitation.

TO MAKE THE BOX

1. Download our Prophecy Wedding Invitation template from our online resources. You will need this for several steps throughout the craft.

2. Using scissors, cut one piece of the 12-by-12-inch cardstock to 10½ by 10½. This will go on the inside of the box.

3. Lay the remaining 12-by-12-inch sheet in front of you, and place a ruler along the top edge. Use a ruler to measure 4 inches from the left side of the paper, and mark that spot with a pencil. Repeat the same process at the 8-inch mark. Turn the ruler 90 degrees so it now lies perpendicular to the top edge of the paper. Place the ruler against the 4-inch mark, and run a bone folder or the corner of a credit card along the length of the ruler, scoring a line down the full length of the paper. Repeat the same process at the 8-inch mark.

4. Turn paper and repeat the process of measuring, marking, and scoring the paper at the 4-inch and 8-inch marks. You should now have nine "boxes" on your paper.

5. Use scissors to cut out the outer corners of the paper so you are left with five boxes and your paper is in the shape of a plus sign. Set aside.

6. Lay the 10½-by-10½-inch paper in front of you, and repeat this process, scoring the paper at the 3¼-inch mark and 7¼-inch mark on both sides. You will have nine boxes here as well, but your center column of boxes will be 4 inches wide, and your side columns of boxes are 3¼ inches wide.

7. Use scissors to cut out the corner boxes from this sheet so that you are left with five boxes and your paper is in the shape of a plus sign. Set aside.

Continued on page 156

8. Fold the scored edges of each box inward toward the center of the box, to make sure they fold and unfold easily.

9. Place double-sided tape or a layer of glue in the center box of the larger piece of paper. Place the smaller sheet on top of the larger one, so the edges of the larger sheet are showing. Press firmly in the center box to attach the two sheets together. The four sides should remain unsecured; this will allow the edges to move more freely, enhancing the "explosive" movement of the box.

TO MAKE THE BOX TOP

10. Print the template for the top portion of the DIY Prophecy Invitation Box on the colored sheet of 8½-by-11-inch cardstock. Use scissors to cut along the solid lines on the pattern; this will give you the square shape. Do not cut along dashed lines; those are for scoring. Note: If your paper is too dark for the lines to show when printed, print the template on lighter paper, cut it out, and use that as a template to trace and cut out your box on the cardstock.

11. Use a bone folder or corner of a credit card to score the paper along the dashed lines. Fold the paper inward toward the center, along the scoring lines.

12. Use scissors to make a small cut along the vertical fold line in the upper left corner, cutting only until you reach the top horizontal fold line. This will turn the left corner of the box into a tab. Turn the paper 90 degrees to the left, and repeat this, cutting tabs into each of the four corners.

13. Fold all the sides inward so they're sticking up. Use double-sided tape or glue to attach each corner tab to the flat edge of the box next to it. This forms the top of the box.

TO MAKE THE INVITATION

14. Open the invitation portion of the DIY Prophecy Wedding Invitations template in Adobe Reader. Fill in the details for your wedding in the editable fields. Print and cut out invitation cards on white cardstock.

15. Use glue or double-side tape to attach the invitation cards to the inside of the box, one for each side.

TO MAKE THE GLOBE

16. Download the Wizard Couple Silhouette from our online resources.

17. If you are using a cutting machine, such as a Cricut, upload the SVG version of the Wizard Couple Silhouette to your design software, and cut on cardstock according to your machine's directions.

18. If you are hand-cutting the design, print the PDF version and cut out.

19. Gently insert the cut design into the fish bowl, with the top of the design pointing toward the dome.

20. If you desire, you could bend the edge of the rectangular base of the couple at a 90-degree angle and glue it to the box layer so that it won't move.

21. Place the globe in the center of the box, gently lift the edges of the box, and place the top on the box.

22. For safety when mailing these invitations, place them in a larger cardboard box, and add bubble wrap or other packing materials so they don't get damaged. Address, stamp, and send by owl post!

FLYING KEY PLACE CARDS

During one of the final scenes in Harry Potter and the Sorcerer's Stone, *Harry searches amid the swarm of flying keys to find "the one"—the key that will open the door and lead them to the next test en route to the Sorcerer's Stone. Inspired by these iconic artifacts, this charming display turns the Flying Keys into place cards, Much like Harry, guests must find "the one"—the key that bears their name and table number so they can find their seat at the reception. We recommend mixing some blank keys into the display for more mystery!*

- Flying Key Place Card template ⬇
- Scissors
- White cardstock
- Hole punch
- Ribbon
- Keys in various sizes and styles

1. Download our Flying Key Place Card template from our online resources.

2. Open the invitation in Adobe Reader. Fill in the guests' names and table numbers on the wings in the editable fields.

3. Print the wings on white cardstock and cut out.

4. Punch a hole in each wing.

5. Use a piece of ribbon to attach two wings— one with the guest's name and one with their table assignment—to a key. Allow extra length of ribbon for hanging the key on a hook or nail for display.

HERMIONE GRANGER:
"CURIOUS. I'VE NEVER SEEN BIRDS LIKE THESE."

HARRY POTTER:
"THEY'RE NOT BIRDS, THEY'RE KEYS. AND I'LL BET ONE OF THEM FITS THAT DOOR."

Harry Potter and the Sorcerer's Stone

"Powerful Love Creates Powerful Magic" Charger Plates & Glasses

Little details come together to make a lasting impression, especially at a wedding. This vinyl template featuring the wedding theme makes it easy to customize your charger plates and glasses for your party.

- "Powerful Love Creates Powerful Magic" vinyl template
- Electric cutting machine (Cricut)
- Adhesive vinyl
- Plates and glassware
- Rubbing alcohol
- Transfer paper

1. Download the "Powerful Love Creates Powerful Magic" vinyl template from our online resources.

2. Using a cutting machine such as a Cricut, upload the SVG version of the design to your design software, and cut according to machine and material directions.

3. Clean the dish surface with rubbing alcohol to make sure nothing will inhibit the vinyl from sticking.

4. Weed the excess vinyl from the quote, and place transfer paper over the text. Use your hand or a credit card to firmly press the transfer paper to your design to ensure it's sticking well, then gently peel the paper away from the original vinyl backing so that the quote adheres to the transfer paper. Apply the cut vinyl design to your dish or glass, then remove the transfer paper.

TIP

Clean the dishes with rubbing alcohol first to make sure no oil or dirt will inhibit the vinyl from adhering to the surface. Washing the finished dishes by hand is recommended to keep them looking their best.

GOLDEN SNITCH KISSING BELLS

There is a charming tradition of ringing a bell to signal a kiss between the couple at weddings. This easy craft turns traditional kissing bells into the Golden Snitch, using jingle bells and white feathers. These fluttering golden bundles are simple to create, and we've included a tag for you to attach to help guests know how to use them! You could place these in a basket at the reception, or place them on the guest tables as a sweet addition to your table décor.

- Golden Snitch Kissing Bells tag ⬇
- Cardstock
- Electric cutting machine such as a Cricut or scissors
- Gold jingle bells in size of your choice (ours were 1 inch)
- White feathers (2 per bell)
- Thin ribbon or miniature clear rubber bands
- White pipe cleaners

1. Download our Golden Snitch Kissing Bells tag from our online resources.

2. If you are using a cutting machine such as a Cricut, upload the PNG version of the design to your design software, and use the Print and Cut feature to print and cut these on cardstock according to your machine's directions.

3. If you are hand-cutting the design, print the PDF version, and cut out the tags.

4. Place one feather on each side of a bell. Run one through the center of the bell so the tip pokes out of the other side. Use a piece of thin ribbon or a small rubber band to carefully tie the tips of the two feathers together, and slide the tied area back into the bell to hide it.

5. Loop the white pipe cleaner through the top of the bell, and slide the tag onto the pipe cleaner. Twist the ends to secure it. The pipe cleaner now becomes the handle for guests to gently shake during the reception.

STYLING MAGIC!

The design basis for the wedding of Bill Weasley and Fleur Delacour in *Harry Potter and the Deathly Hallows – Part 1* was the tent the party was held in: a pale gray marquee with a purple interior. The production design team decided that since Fleur's parents were probably helping cover the cost of the wedding, it is likely they would have had a strong say in the décor and that permitted a French influence, which was decidedly "un-Weasley-ish." The décor included, in Stuart Craig's words, "a refined soft interior, painted silks, and floating candles in eighteenth-century French style candelabra." There were also black faux bamboo chairs, purple tablecloths, carpets, and flowers, as well as black butterflies, added by the visual effects team in postproduction, which flitted around the tent poles. After completing the scene, set decorator Stephenie McMillan declared she never wanted to do another wedding design. "It's too stressful!"

Each couple's wedding should be styled to match their own tastes and preferences, and the individual components of this reception can be adapted easily to suit a number of styles, from sophisticated to rustic. A few key props and décor items that will help you re-create the rustic, natural style of the reception pictured in these pages are trunks, bird cages, large pillar candles, burlap fabric, crocheted table dressings, and, of course, lots of flowers.

ABOVE: Concept art of Bill and Fleur's wedding by Andrew Williamson for *Harry Potter and the Deathly Hallows – Part 1*.

Deathly Hallows Wreath

One of the most iconic symbols in the film, the triangular mark of the Deathly Hallows, represents three powerful magical artifacts: the Elder Wand, the Resurrection Stone, and the Cloak of Invisibility. This easy DIY wreath offers a rustic, natural take on this classic symbol that adds an elegant touch to any aspect of your celebration.

- Small branches, about 24 to 30 inches long, collected in nature or purchased at a craft store
- Small grapevine wreath, 7 to 8 inches in diameter
- Jute twine
- Floral wire (optional)
- Chopstick
- Hot-glue gun
- Brown paint
- Tacky glue (optional)
- Small decorative white owl figure (optional)
- Artificial floral berries
- Artificial vines or moss
- Artificial natural accents such as grass, wood, flowers, leaves

1. Using the small branches you collected outside, create a triangular shape with the small grapevine wreath in the center to help you size it. The sides of the triangle should touch the outside of the wreath. Use two to four branches on each side of the triangle.

2. Use the twine to lash each corner of the triangle together. Make sure to leave some extra branch to give the wreath a more natural feel.

3. Using either floral wire or jute twine, connect the triangle to the wreath.

"THE ELDER WAND, THE MOST POWERFUL WAND EVER MADE, THE RESURRECTION STONE, THE CLOAK OF INVISIBILITY. TOGETHER, THEY MAKE THE DEATHLY HALLOWS. TOGETHER, THEY MAKE ONE MASTER OF DEATH. BUT FEW TRULY BELIEVE THAT SUCH OBJECTS EXIST. . . ."

Xenophilius Lovegood, *Harry Potter and the Deathly Hallows – Part 1*

4. Make your own Elder Wand using the large chopstick and hot glue. Using your glue gun, create little balls of glue a few inches apart getting smaller as you go to the top of the wand. To make this easier, spin the wand as you put glue on—it helps to create the ball shape. Continue to spin the wand until the glue is mostly dry before you make your next ball.

5. Once the hot glue is dry, paint your Elder Wand a dark brown.

6. Glue your wand (with either tacky glue or hot glue) to the center of your triangle and circle combo to create the Deathly Hallows symbol.

7. Glue your little white owl to the bottom left corner of your wreath, if using.

8. On the bottom right corner of the wreath, lay out your artificial flower elements, and arrange until they fit with your style. Attach what you can with floral wire or jute twine. Glue down everything else.

9. You can hang as is if you have a small door hook. If not, create a small loop out of jute twine and attach to the back of your wreath using glue. Hang your wreath from a nail or over-the-door hanger.

MIRROR OF ERISED WELCOME MESSAGE

When exploring the castle in his first year at Hogwarts, Harry discovers the mystical Mirror of Erised and comes face to face with that which he most desires: his loving parents. Inspired by the mirror's power, you can share a similarly sentimental message with your wedding guests, declaring, "We desire nothing more than to celebrate our love today with you." An electric cutting machine such as a Cricut makes it easy to re-create this message with vinyl applied to a gold-framed mirror. Place the mirror at the front of your reception as a gorgeous backdrop to your welcome table.

- Mirror of Erised Welcome Message ⊙
- Gold vinyl
- Gold-framed mirror
- Transfer paper

1. Download our Mirror of Erised Welcome Message from our online resources.

2. Using a cutting machine like a Cricut, upload the SVG files to your design software. Cut the message according to your machine's directions on gold vinyl.

3. Make sure your mirror's surface is clean and dry. Weed the excess vinyl from the quote and place transfer paper over the text. Use your hand or a credit card to firmly press the transfer paper to your design to ensure it's sticking well, then gently peel the paper away from the original vinyl backing so that the quote adheres to the transfer paper. Apply the cut vinyl design to your mirror, then remove the transfer paper.

4. Set up your mirror behind your welcome station to greet your guests.

BEHIND THE MAGIC

The writing that appears over the biggest arch of the Mirror of Erised reads: ERISED STRA EHRU OYT UBE CAFRU OYT ON WOHSI. It's not a magical language, but rather the mirror image of the sentence, "I show not your face but your heart's desire," with the letters appearing backward. Unlike most props, which are duplicated for different uses and in case of breakage during filming, due to its size and complexity, only one Mirror of Erised was ever created for the films.

Owl Post Gift Station

Owl post is a wizard's preferred method of sending messages, and here this Owl Post Gift Station becomes a charming receptacle for guests to pass along their love notes and gifts to the couple. The board is covered with copies of Harry's letter from Hogwarts, which flood the Dursley home in Harry Potter and the Sorcerer's Stone, *and then topped with a printable Owl Post sign. You can print this sign in two pieces and attach it together, or take it to your local print shop to have it printed in one continuous piece, as you choose. An old travel suitcase or trunk sets an endearing tone and provides a lovely base for this display.*

- Letter from Hogwarts Envelope printable ⬤
- Owl Post Gift Station Banner printable ⬤
- Large poster board (size will depend on your station)
- White printer paper
- White cardstock
- Scissors
- Double-sided tape
- Trunk or suitcase, if desired for base

1. Download our Letter from Hogwarts Envelope and Owl Post Gift Station Banner printables from our online resources.

2. Print as many copies of the envelope (both front and back) on printer paper as you need to cover your poster board.

3. Print the Owl Post sign on cardstock. We have provided two versions of this, one sized for standard letter-size paper, which you can print and piece together yourself, or a larger file size you can have your local print center create for you. Cut out the banner to reveal the shape.

4. Attach the envelopes to the poster board with double-sided tape. Hang them at different angles and allow them to overlap a little to create a haphazard flying effect. Incorporate some of the back side of the envelope for extra visual interest.

5. Once your board is covered, attach the Owl Post banner in the center of the board.

6. Set up the board inside an open suitcase or trunk at your gift station. Style with additional trunks, cases, and an open birdcage for letters and cards.

TRIWIZARD CHARCUTERIE BOARD

According to Hermione Granger, the Triwizard Tournament is all about international magical cooperation between the Hogwarts students and those from Beauxbatons Academy of Magic and the Durmstrang Institute. We think this charcuterie board does a sensational job of mixing and mingling many of the best and most beloved foods of each region in an international culinary cooperation. The perfect cheese board for any elegant occasion, use our selections as a springboard and then customize this to your personal preferences for your own board.

YIELD: 6 TO 8 SERVINGS

FOR HOGWARTS

Meat: salt-cured ham

Cheeses: cheddar, Double Gloucester, Stilton, or Havarti

Sides: pickled onions, apple slices, Branston pickles

FOR BEAUXBATONS

Meats: pâtés or terrines

Cheeses: Camembert, Brie, Gruyère

Sides: grapes, honey, almonds, olives

FOR DURMSTRANG

Meats: Swedish meatballs, smoked sausage, liver pâté, smoked salmon, pickled herring

Sides: sliced onions, capers, sour cream, pickled red cabbage

Arrange meats and cheeses on charcuterie tray.

Add in other elements to fill in gaps and create a lush board.

Portraits of Scabbers Cheeseboard

Inspired by Ron's pet rat, this fun recipe uses sliced almonds and raisins to turn small triangular cheese wedges into miniature portraits of Scabbers. We recommend serving this alongside the Triwizard Charcuterie Board as this is the perfect cheesy option for younger guests who haven't yet developed the taste for Camembert or pâté.

Yield: approximately 4 servings

8 ounces English cheddar cheese
8 ounces Brie
8 ounces Gorgonzola
16 pieces sliced almonds
¼ cup raisins
16 crackers (4 per plate)

Slice cheese into small triangle shapes, reserving scraps.

Cut remaining scraps of cheese into very thin "whisker" shapes. Set aside.

Use a small paring knife to make a slice on each side of the wide end of the small cheese triangles. Insert one sliced almond for ears into each slice.

Cut raisins into small pieces and roll between your fingers to make the pieces round. Place them as eyes on top of the cheese triangle, and one piece at the tip of the triangle as a nose.

Using a toothpick, poke a hole into the sides of the narrow end of the triangle, and again using the toothpick, press the cheese "whiskers" into the holes.

Serve with crackers.

Bezoar Bruschetta

As Harry learns in Harry Potter and the Half-Blood Prince, *bezoars are stones taken from the stomachs of goats which serve as powerful antidotes to most poisons. They also happen to look quite a bit like dried figs, which forms the basis of inspiration for this sweet and sophisticated starter. While this bruschetta will not counteract the effects of poisoned mead, it will give hungry guests something tasty to sample while waiting for the couple's grand entrance during cocktail hour.*

Yield: 6 slices

1 tablespoon olive oil
6 slices of French bread
6 ounces goat cheese
6 dried or fresh figs, sliced
Lemon thyme, for garnish
Honey, drizzle for garnish

Heat a grill pan over medium heat so it is hot and ready for grilling.

Brush olive oil on French bread and grill bread in a grill pan over medium heat for 2 to 3 minutes.

Remove from heat and spread goat cheese on French bread slices.

Top with sliced figs and garnish with lemon thyme and honey.

Serve immediately.

Professor Sprout's Signature Salad

Make Professor Sprout proud! Serve this salad, filled with an impressive array of vegetables and herbs, to your guests, and let them see how many they can identify to determine if they have the skills to assist in the Hogwarts greenhouses.

Yield: 4 servings

FOR THE DRESSING

¼ cup fresh basil
1 small clove garlic, minced
½ shallot, minced
1½ tablespoons fresh lemon juice
1½ tablespoons white wine vinegar
2 tablespoons extra-virgin olive oil
1 tablespoon Parmesan cheese, grated
¼ teaspoon salt

FOR THE SALAD

1 bunch asparagus, chopped
3 cups spring greens
½ cup fresh shelled peas
2 to 3 radishes, sliced
1 avocado, pitted and sliced (drizzle with lemon juice to keep from turning color)
1 cup heirloom cherry tomatoes, halved
½ cup canned chickpeas
½ cup sesame seeds
Fresh herbs, such as mint, basil, chives, for garnish

TO MAKE THE DRESSING

Place all dressing ingredients in a blender, or a jar with a top, and blend or shake to combine. Set dressing aside to allow the flavors to mingle.

TO MAKE THE SALAD

Prepare an ice bath. Bring a large pot of water to a boil, and blanch the asparagus for 1 minute or until just tender. Transfer to the ice bath for 1 minute to stop the cooking process. Drain in a colander.

Place asparagus in a large bowl, and add spring greens, peas, radishes, avocado, tomatoes, chickpeas, sesame seeds, and herbs.

Add half the dressing to the salad, and toss to coat. Reserve half the dressing to serve with the salad.

Serve immediately.

SORCERER'S STONE ALCHEMICAL BACON-WRAPPED POTATOES

The Sorcerer's Stone is a magical gem that grants immortality to anyone who possesses it. Inspired by the stone's delicate size and rich red color, these potatoes won't make you immortal, but they will leave you with a full belly!

YIELD: 20 TO 25 PIECES

¼ cup granulated sugar
½ tablespoon kosher salt
1 tablespoon paprika
½ teaspoon ground cayenne
8 ounces bacon, each strip cut into thirds
1 pound (20 to 25) small one-bite potatoes

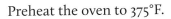

Preheat the oven to 375°F.

In a medium bowl, combine the sugar, salt, and spices. Mix thoroughly. Set aside.

Line a rimmed baking sheet with foil, and place a wire rack on it.

Working with several pieces at a time, dredge the bacon in the sugar mixture until it is well coated.

Wrap each potato in a piece of bacon, making sure it is covered on all sides, and secure with a toothpick.

Place each wrapped potato on the wire rack. Bake for 25 to 30 minutes, or until bacon is crispy and the potatoes are fork tender. Serve immediately.

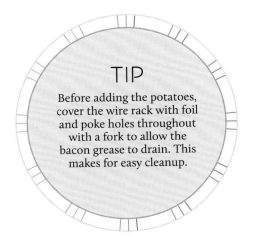

TIP

Before adding the potatoes, cover the wire rack with foil and poke holes throughout with a fork to allow the bacon grease to drain. This makes for easy cleanup.

"I SEE MYSELF HOLDING THE STONE. BUT HOW DO I GET IT?"

Quirinus Quirrell, *Harry Potter and the Sorcerer's Stone*

Sign of the Hallows Rosemary Shrimp Skewers

The Deathly Hallows is made up of three incredibly powerful magical objects: the Elder Wand, the Resurrection Stone, and the Cloak of Invisibility. First introduced in Harry Potter and the Deathly Hallows – Part 1, *the Hallows are represented by a triangular symbol with a circle and line through the middle. This elegant recipe uses simple styling to re-create the iconic symbol of the Hallows, making this entrée a magical centerpiece for any table.*

Yield: 6 servings as an entrée; 12 as an appetizer

FOR THE VINAIGRETTE

4 tablespoons olive oil
1 tablespoon white wine vinegar
Juice of 1 lemon
1 teaspoon salt
1 clove garlic, minced
1 teaspoon minced fresh rosemary
1 tablespoon honey
Fresh ground black pepper

FOR THE SHRIMP SKEWERS

¼ cup lemon juice
¼ teaspoon red pepper flakes
½ teaspoon kosher salt
2 tablespoons honey
2 tablespoons olive oil
1½ pounds 26/30 count fresh shrimp
12 to 16 long sprigs fresh rosemary

TO MAKE THE VINAIGRETTE

In a small bowl, whisk all the ingredients together. Set aside until ready to serve.

TO MAKE THE SHRIMP SKEWERS

Preheat the oven to 350°F. In a large bowl, whisk all the marinade ingredients together. Add the shrimp, and toss to thoroughly coat. Let marinate for 20 minutes.

While the shrimp are marinating, strip the leaves off the bottom of each rosemary skewer, exposing 4 to 6 inches.

Add 2 to 3 shrimp to each skewer, making sure to catch both ends of each shrimp with the skewer.

Place the skewers on a rimmed baking sheet, and bake for 10 to 15 minutes until the shrimp are opaque and firm.

TO SERVE

Place a bowl of the vinaigrette in the middle of a rustic cutting board. Arrange the skewers around the bowl in the shape a triangle, making sure to alternate the direction of the skewers. Add a long spoon to the bowl to mimic the Elder Wand in the center of the symbol. Serve immediately.

Professor Lockhart's Five-Time Award-Winning Most Charming Lasagna Rolls

Inspired by the outrageous Professor Lockhart and his ruffly dandy outfits, we've taken traditional lasagna rolls and given them a makeover we think the flamboyant professor would heartily approve of.

1 cup walnuts

1 cup fresh parsley leaves

1 teaspoon sea salt, divided

1½ cups grated Parmesan, divided

2 tablespoons white truffle oil

16 ounces dried lasagna noodles

2 tablespoons olive oil, divided

½ cup (1 stick) unsalted butter, divided, plus more for pan

3 cloves garlic, minced

4 tablespoons flour

2 cups half-and-half

12 ounces wild mushrooms, such as shiitake, oyster, hen of the woods, or beech

16 ounces whole-milk ricotta

8 ounces fresh mozzarella, sliced

Fresh parsley, for garnish (optional)

Process walnuts, parsley leaves, and half a teaspoon of sea salt in a food processor until they resemble fine crumbs.

In a medium bowl, mix the parsley-walnut mixture with 1 cup of the Parmesan and the truffle oil. Set aside.

Heat a large pot filled with salted water and one tablespoon of olive oil over medium-high. Add the lasagna noodles, and cook until al dente, about 12 minutes. Stir them gently as they cook to avoid sticking. Drain the noodles and transfer them to a large bowl. Toss with the remaining tablespoon of olive oil.

Make the béchamel: Melt 4 tablespoons of butter in a medium saucepan. Add the garlic and the rest of the salt, and sauté for 2 to 3 minutes, until fragrant. Sprinkle the flour on top of the garlic, stirring to combine, and cook another 2 to 3 minutes, until just golden brown. Slowly add half-and-half, and stir until smooth. Cook 3 to 5 minutes more until the sauce thickens and coats the back of the spoon. Remove from heat, cover, and set aside.

Add the remaining 4 tablespoons of butter to a large sauté pan over medium heat. When it begins to foam, add the mushrooms, and stir to coat them with the butter. Once the mushrooms are well-coated, allow them to sit in a single layer, stirring occasionally, until they are nice and brown, 5 to 7 minutes. Remove from the heat.

Add the ricotta to the walnut mixture, and stir to combine.

To assemble the dish, lightly butter a 3-quart lasagna pan. Spread half a cup of the béchamel in an even layer on the bottom.

Working with one noodle at a time, spread a generous 2 tablespoons of ricotta filling on the noodle. Sprinkle a mounded

tablespoon of mushrooms on top of the filling. Place two or three slices of mozzarella toward the center of the noodle. Roll up the noodle and place seam side down in the lasagna pan. Continue working until the pan is full (you may have an extra noodle or two left over).

Pour the remaining sauce over the noodles, and sprinkle the remaining Parmesan over the top. Bake for 25 to 30 minutes or until bubbly and golden brown on top. Garnish with chopped parsley if desired, and serve immediately.

Letter from Hogwarts Jam Pastries

The Hogwarts Acceptance Letter is one of the most iconic props from the first film and possibly the whole series. Here we have reimagined it in the sweetest form yet, as a delicious pastry bursting with a jam of your choice. For the most authentic result, use a Hogwarts wax stamp to "seal" the letters in red candy melts. Guests will flock to get one of their own pastry letters when you serve these flaky tarts.

Yield: 8 tarts

FOR THE SEALS

12 red candy melts

Ice water

1 to 2 tablespoons butter, softened

FOR THE PASTRY

2½ cups flour

½ cup powdered sugar

1 teaspoon kosher salt

¾ cup (1½ sticks) unsalted butter, very cold

¼ cup vegetable shortening, very cold

6 tablespoons water

Ice

1 cup jam, in the flavor of your choice

1 egg, lightly beaten with 1 tablespoon water, for egg wash

SPECIAL SUPPLIES

2 or more Hogwarts wax stamps

TO MAKE THE SEALS

Preheat the oven to 200°F. Place 12 candy melts well-spaced onto a parchment-lined cookie sheet. Reserve the remaining candy melts to glue each wax seal to your pastry tart. Have a second cookie sheet standing by.

Set up your workstation. Fill a bowl with ice water, and place the wax stamps inside it. Have a paper towel and the butter close at hand. To make things go faster, use two or more stamps, and keep any not in use in the water.

Place the cookie sheet with the candy melts in the oven for 1½ to 2 minutes until the melts are shiny and beginning to melt, but still hold their shape. Remove the sheet from the oven, and slip the parchment onto the cool cookie sheet. Allow melts to rest 2 to 3 minutes so they set a bit. Turn off the oven.

Pull a stamp from the ice water, grease the paper towel with a bit of butter, and wipe down the stamp, removing water droplets and greasing slightly. Press the seal firmly into the center of a candy melt, and allow it to sit undisturbed 45 seconds to 1½ minutes. When the stamp is ready to be removed, it will twist off from the candy melt.

Place the stamp back in the ice water for about 30 seconds, or if using multiple stamps, select a fresh one to do the next seal. Seals that do not turn out as desired can be returned to the oven and remelted. The candy seals can be made up to a week in advance and stored in airtight container.

Continued on page 178

TO MAKE THE PASTRY

Combine all the dry ingredients.

Use a pastry cutter to cut the butter and shortening into the flour mixture until it resembles a coarse crumb with no pieces bigger than a pea.

Pour the water over ice and allow to sit for 1 minute (you want the water to be very cold). Pour about half the ice water over the flour-butter mixture, and use the pastry cutter to blend until shaggy dough comes together. Add a bit more water as needed to bring all the flour into the dough. Split the dough in half, wrap both halves in parchment paper, and allow to rest in the refrigerator 30 minutes.

Roll out one disk of dough to a 9-by-14-inch rectangle, and trim to square it up, reserving scraps. With a sharp knife or a pastry wheel, cut the dough into 8 "envelope" pieces about 3 inches by 4½ inches. Refrigerate these pieces while repeating the process with the other disk of dough. Refrigerate all the pieces for 15 minutes.

Roll out the scraps, and use them to cut 8 triangle-shaped pieces, with a long side of about 4 inches. Working with pairs of rectangular pieces, brush the edges with egg wash and place 2 tablespoons of jam in the center of a bottom piece. Place a second piece on top. Crimp the edges all the way around with a fork. Brush the entire envelope with egg wash, and place a triangle on top against one of the long edges, stretching gently if necessary. Crimp along the joined edge with the fork to seal. Brush the triangle with egg wash. Using a paring knife, cut a small slit directly under the point of the triangle. Once assembled, refrigerate for another 15 minutes while you preheat the oven to 400°F.

Bake for 20 to 25 minutes or until golden brown and crisp. When the pastries are cool, melt the leftover candy melts and use as glue to attach the seals.

ABOVE: Number four, Privet Drive is flooded with letters from Hogwarts in *Harry Potter and the Sorcerer's Stone.*

Making the Letter From Hogwarts Jam Pastries

THREE BROOMSTICKS
BUTTERSCOTCH PUDDING

The Three Broomsticks is a popular pub in Hogsmeade, the wizarding village within walking distance to Hogwarts. Inspired by the Butterbeer served in the pub, this creamy butterscotch pudding, served in clear glass mugs and topped with a mountain of whipped cream, is a velvety sweet treat your guests won't be able to refuse!

Yield: 8 servings

FOR THE PUDDING

3 tablespoons cornstarch
2½ cups whole milk, divided
1 cup dark brown sugar
2 tablespoons bourbon (or vanilla extract)
½ cup (1 stick) unsalted butter
1 cup heavy cream
1 tablespoon vanilla extract
¼ teaspoon salt
¼ teaspoon allspice

FOR THE WHIPPED CREAM

½ cup heavy cream
1 tablespoon powdered sugar
½ tablespoon vanilla extract
1 cup toffee chips, divided

SPECIAL SUPPLIES

Pastry bag with star tip

TO MAKE THE PUDDING

In a small bowl or measuring cup, mix 3 tablespoons cornstarch with ½ cup of milk. Set aside.

Add the brown sugar and bourbon to a medium saucepan, and cook over medium heat until the sugar is melted and beginning to bubble. Add butter, and continue to cook, stirring until the butter is melted and incorporated. Bring the mixture to a boil and let cook while stirring occasionally until the mixture darkens and becomes fragrant, up to 5 minutes.

Gradually add cream to butterscotch mixture. Stir until butterscotch is dissolved into cream. Add the remaining 2 cups of milk, salt, allspice, and the vanilla, and stir to combine.

Remove the saucepan from heat, and add cornstarch-milk mixture. Return to heat on medium-high, and cook, stirring constantly until it barely comes to a simmer and begins to thicken. Cook for 1 minute more, and remove from heat.

Divide the pudding among 8 glasses, leaving plenty of room for whipped cream. Cover the surface of each pudding with a square of wax paper, and refrigerate at least 4 hours or overnight.

TO MAKE THE WHIPPED CREAM

In a large bowl, use a hand mixer to whip the cream, sugar, and vanilla together on high speed until stiff peaks form (you can also do this by hand). Fold in half a cup of the toffee chips, reserving the rest for garnish.

TO SERVE

Using a pastry bag fitted with a large star attachment, pipe the whipped cream onto each pudding. Pile it high and let it "foam" over the side. Sprinkle each pudding with the remaining toffee chips. Serve immediately.

PATRONUS CHARM PULL CAKE

The tradition of ribbon charm pulling dates back to the 1600s and has always signified good luck at a wedding. Decorated to look like the forest where Harry first sees the Doe Patronus, this stunning cake gives the tradition a Harry Potter twist by using silver animal charms attached to ribbons to signify different Patronuses. Once the cake is baked and decorated, tuck your "Patronus charms" under the base of the cake, with the ribbon hanging out. The bridal party or guests can then pull the charms during the reception to reveal their Patronus!

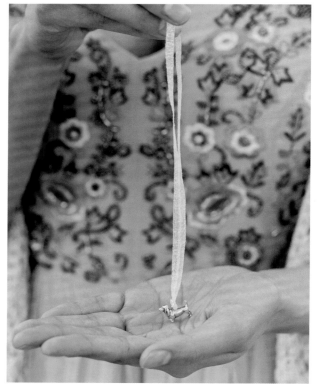

YIELD: 12 TO 16 SERVINGS

FOR THE CAKE

3⅓ cups flour
2¼ teaspoons baking powder
¾ teaspoon baking soda
¼ teaspoon salt
1 cup (2 sticks) unsalted butter
2¼ cups sugar
2 teaspoons vanilla
2 teaspoons lemon zest
4 eggs
½ cup lemon juice
1 cup Greek yogurt

FOR THE WHITE CHOCOLATE MOUSSE FILLING

¾ teaspoon gelatin
3 tablespoons cold water
8 ounces white chocolate
1½ cups heavy cream, divided

FOR THE BUTTERCREAM

⅔ cup pasteurized egg whites
1½ cups sugar
2 cups (4 sticks) butter, softened, cut into tablespoon-sized pieces
1 teaspoon vanilla

FOR DECORATING

Two 13½-ounce containers Pirouette cookies
6 ounces white chocolate
Sparkle sugar

SPECIAL SUPPLIES

Stag and Doe Patronus Cake Topper templates ⊙
Offset spatula
9-inch round cake board or serving plate
Printer paper
Up to 16 silver animal charms on 12-inch ribbons

TIP
You can buy simple silver animal charms online or from most craft stores.

TO MAKE THE CAKES

Preheat the oven to 350°F. Prepare two 8-inch cake pans by lining the bottom with parchment.

In a medium bowl, mix all the dry ingredients together. Set aside.

In the bowl of a stand mixer fitted with a paddle attachment, beat the butter and sugar together on paddle speed until light and fluffy. Add in the eggs, one at a time, scraping down the sides after each addition. Add the vanilla and lemon zest.

In a small bowl, mix the lemon juice with the Greek yogurt.

Starting with about a third of the dry mixture, alternate between adding the dry ingredients and the yogurt mixture to the bowl of the stand mixer. Mix well on medium speed, and scrape down the sides of the bowl after each addition.

Divide the batter evenly between the two pans, and bake for 30 to 35 minutes or until a cake tester comes out clean. Rotate the cakes halfway through the cooking time.

Allow cakes to cool in the pan on a wire rack for 15 minutes. Gently work an offset spatula between the cake and the pan to loosen the edge and then turn out onto the wire rack to cool completely.

TO MAKE THE WHITE MOUSSE FILLING

In a small bowl, let gelatin bloom over cold water.

Add white chocolate to a medium heatproof bowl.

In a small saucepan, heat half a cup of the cream until just scalding, 3 to 5 minutes. Add the gelatin mixture, and stir until dissolved.

Pour the cream mixture over white chocolate, and allow to stand 5 minutes. Stir to completely melt chocolate so the mixture is completely smooth. Run the mixture through a fine sieve if there is any undissolved gelatin.

In the bowl of a stand mixer fitted with a whisk attachment, whip the remaining cup of heavy cream on high speed until stiff peaks form.

Fold the white chocolate mixture into the whipped cream, and chill for at least 2 hours.

TO MAKE THE BUTTERCREAM

Place a heatproof measuring cup or bowl inside a saucepan. Fill the saucepan with water until the water level reaches halfway up the cup. Remove the measuring cup, and turn the heat to medium. Bring the water to a simmer.

In the measuring cup, combine the egg white with the sugar, and whisk until blended. Place the measuring cup into the simmering water and heat, stirring constantly, until the sugar is completely dissolved and the mixture is hot.

Carefully remove the measuring cup containing the sugar-egg mixture from the saucepan, and transfer the mixture to the bowl of a stand mixer fitted with a whisk attachment. Whisk the egg white and sugar mixture on high until completely cool. The mixture should be white and opaque, with elastic ribbons flowing from the beater—a loose, sticky meringue. This could take 7 to 10 minutes.

Add the softened butter to the meringue one piece at a time with the mixer on low, until all the butter is incorporated.

Add vanilla, and turn up the mixer to medium, mix until smooth, 1 to 2 minutes more.

TO ASSEMBLE AND DECORATE THE CAKE

Using a sharp knife, cut your cake rounds in half through the middle, creating four layers of cake, 8 inches in diameter.

Fill a pastry bag with about a cup of buttercream. Cut an opening in the tip and have standing by.

Working on a cake board or serving plate, smear a small amount of buttercream on the board, and place the bottom layer of the cake over it. Use the piping bag to pipe a "wall" of buttercream around the edge of the layer. Fill with about a cup of chilled white chocolate mousse.

Repeat this process to create two more layers of cake and mousse. Place the fourth layer on top to finish the cake. Chill the cake for 30 minutes.

Using an offset spatula and the remaining buttercream, frost the entire cake. Keep in mind that the side will be covered in cookies and doesn't need to be perfect. At this point, the cake can be refrigerated for up to 24 hours. If the cake has been refrigerated, allow it to come to room temperature for 20 to 30 minutes before decorating.

Download the Stag and Doe Patronus Cake Topper templates from our online resources and print on printer paper.

Lay out all the cookies on parchment-lined cookie sheets, and cover your Patronus templates with squares of parchment.

In a microwave-safe bowl, melt the white chocolate in 30-second bursts, stirring between each one. Once the chocolate is melted, place it in a pastry bag, and cut a small hole in the tip.

Trace the stag and doe in the white chocolate, and fill in. Sprinkle immediately with sparkle sugar. Drizzle the remaining white chocolate over all the cookies and sprinkle with more sparkle sugar. Allow to set for 5 to 10 minutes.

Press the cookies into the sides of the cake, breaking them at different lengths to create a staggered look. Once all the cookies are on the cake, scrape up the remaining chocolate and sugar from the parchment and sprinkle it on top of the cake.

Carefully remove the stag and doe from the parchment, and use leftover cookie pieces to stand them up in the center of the cake.

Tuck each charm under the edge of the cake board leaving the ribbons hanging out. The cake can sit out for 4 hours without refrigeration. When ready to serve, have each guest or member of the bridal party grasp the end of one ribbon and pull. This will choose their Patronus. Make sure your guests or bridal party pulls all the charms before cutting the cake!

ABOVE: Concept art of the Doe Patronus by Andrew Williamson for *Harry Potter and the Deathly Hallows – Part 1.*

QUIDDITCH BEAN BAG TOSS

Bean bag games have become a beloved cocktail hour pastime at weddings, especially as a way for guests to stay entertained while couples are off having their photos taken. We've added a Harry Potter spin to this fun activity inspired by the wizarding world's own beloved sport: Quidditch!

- Quidditch Bean Bag Toss pattern ⊙
- Adhesive vinyl
- Transfer paper
- Electric cutting machine such as a Cricut or scissors
- Plain wooden cornhole set
- Sandpaper (optional)
- Paint in colors of your choosing, such as sky blue, white, and gold

1. Download our Quidditch Bean Bag Toss pattern from our online resources.

2. If you are using a cutting machine such as a Cricut, upload the SVG version of the design to your design software, and cut the vinyl pattern according to machine and material directions. You will need two versions of the pattern, one for each board.

3. If you are hand-cutting the design, print the PDF version, and cut it out, then use the cutout as your pattern to cut out the final design from the vinyl.

4. Prepare your board. If your board has any kind of stain or sealant, you may need to scuff it with sandpaper before painting to help the paint stick. Paint the board sky blue, and add any extra details you like: clouds, the sun, a fluttering Golden Snitch, a Hogwarts Quidditch player on his broom, even a Dementor if you're feeling spooky. Note: This is work best done outside on a drop cloth to avoid mess. Leave the boards outside to dry overnight or until completely dry.

5. Weed the excess vinyl from the pattern, and place transfer paper over the image. Use your hand or a credit card to firmly press the transfer paper to your design to ensure it's sticking well, then gently peel the paper away from the original vinyl backing so the quote adheres to the transfer paper.

6. Apply the cut vinyl design to your board, then remove the transfer paper. Repeat with the second board.

TIP
Plain wooden cornhole sets are readily available online and in some specialty stores.

Mrs. Weasley's Homemade Jam Jars With Labels

Molly Weasley is a dynamo homemaker whose love for her family, crafty creativity, and handmade aesthetic is perceivable in every aspect of her character, from her costume to the set dressing in her home to the small touches you may not even notice on-screen. One example of this is the adorable labels the graphics department created for her homemade jams and preserves. Jam, whether homemade or not, makes an excellent favor, and with the addition of Mrs. Weasley's labels, you'll be able to send guests home with a sweet thank-you with a warm Weasley touch.

- Mrs. Weasley's Homemade Jam labels ⬇
- Cardstock or full-page shipping label sheets
- Scissors
- Jam jars
- Fabric circles and ribbon (optional)

1. Download Mrs. Weasley's Homemade Jam labels from our online resources.

2. Print out on cardstock or on full-page shipping label sheets.

3. Cut out and attach to jam jars.

4. Fill the jars with your favorite homemade jam or store-bought preserves.

5. You could add a circle of calico fabric to the top, secured with ribbon to complete the homespun look!

A Glossary of Basic Cooking Terms, Techniques, and Ingredients

TECHNIQUES

BLANCH

Blanching is a quick-cooking technique where you plunge vegetables into boiling water for a short period of time and then immediately immerse them in ice-cold water to preserve their peak crunch and taste.

BLOOMING GELATIN

When working with gelatin, it is vital to sprinkle the powdered gelatin in liquid and allow it to sit and "bloom" for 3 to 5 minutes. Then, when the mixture is heated, the gelatin will dissolve evenly. This will ensure a smooth texture in your finished dish.

CUTTING IN BUTTER

This term relates to working large chunks of very cold butter into dry ingredients such as flour in order to break the butter down into smaller pieces that are fully coated and incorporated into the dry ingredients. The result is a crumb-like mixture with a texture like wet sand. Typically a pastry cutter is used to help this process go faster.

DEEP-FRYING

Don't be frightened! Deep-frying is not as nerve-racking as it sounds. To set up your deep-frying station, place a Dutch oven or large, high-sided pan on the burner.* Clip a fry thermometer to the side and fill with enough oil to submerge your food. You want to use an oil with a high smoke point, such as canola, safflower, or peanut. With the heat on medium-high or high, slowly bring your oil up to the temperature called for in the recipe. Keep an eye on this as you're cooking; the oil temp will change when you add food, and you may need to take some time to bring it back up to temp between batches.

A few safety tips: When frying food in hot oil, remember to never leave the pan unattended, and keep a close eye on the time and color of the food you are cooking. Not only can food burn quickly in oil if it is left in too long, but it can also become a fire hazard. When adding food to hot oil, be sure to use tongs and protective cooking mitts if necessary. Always place food in the oil, as opposed to dropping it. This will help avoid splashes and splatters, which can cause severe burns. It is also good when removing food to place it on a paper-towel-lined plate to help remove excess cooking oils and help your food stay crisp. Please note deep frying should only be done by an adult; if children are present, adult supervision is necessary at all times when oil is heating or hot.

*You can, of course, use a deep fryer instead of a Dutch oven on the stove if you have one.

FLOODING ICING

A technique for achieving bakery-worthy results when icing cookies. First pipe a stiff line of icing along the edge of the cookie, then use a slightly runnier icing to fill in the outline, covering the cookies completely. Finally, use a scribe tool or a toothpick to smooth out any inconsistencies or air bubbles.

ICE BATH

An ice bath is used to quickly cool down hot food, particularly after blanching. To prepare an ice bath, simply fill a large bowl with ice and cold water. You may need to stir the food you put in the ice bath to help the cold distribute evenly throughout the cooling process.

SACHET

In cooking terms, a sachet, also known as a bouquet garni or spice sachet, is a little bundle of porous material that holds spices and herbs for infusing. Intended to be removed before serving, these are used when you want to add flavor to a dish but don't want a lot of loose herbs and spices floating around in the finished product. They can be made by placing your ingredients in the center of a piece of kitchen gauze, cheesecloth, or a fabric tea filter bag and then tying it off with kitchen twine.

SUPPLIES & EQUIPMENT

COOKIE SCOOP

A cookie scoop is a spring-loaded scoop-shaped tool often used for measuring batter and dough. These come in a variety of sizes and can be used to create even, round portions of all kind of doughs, batters, and mixes. In larger sizes, these are sometimes listed as ice-cream scoops.

DUTCH OVEN

A Dutch oven is a heavy cooking pot often made of cast iron that is ideal for making stews or deep-frying, because it will hold and distribute heat evenly. It works well with high or low temperatures and is a versatile cooking tool that is a handy addition to every kitchen.

FRY THERMOMETER

A frying thermometer helps you measure the temperature of oils in recipes where precise temperatures are critical. A candy thermometer works in the same way and can be used here. They are made of a thick glass that can handle the heat and often have a clip on the side that you can attach to your pot so you don't have to hold it while you are waiting for your oil to reach the appropriate temperature.

KITCHEN SHEARS

Beyond just a pair of scissors, kitchen shears typically have a plastic or rubber handle, and the blades include a special notch for cutting poultry joints. Oftentimes they come with a feature that allows you to fully separate the individual shears for thorough cleaning. For hygiene purposes, these should never be substituted for craft scissors.

MANDOLINE

A mandoline is a kitchen tool used for quickly slicing vegetables into even, uniform slices. Please note the blade on a mandoline is extremely sharp, so be careful when using so you don't accidentally slice your hand. If you don't have a mandolin, you can use a very sharp chef's knife, however your slices will likely be thicker than you would get with a mandolin.

PASTRY CUTTER

This is a handheld kitchen tool with metal tines used for cutting cold butter into dry ingredients quickly and easily. Best of all, the tines are curved, making it easy to use the tool right in your mixing bowl. If you don't have a pastry cutter, you can use a fork or knife to work the butter into your ingredients.

STAND MIXER

This is an electronic kitchen tool made up of a mixing bowl and various attachments. These are most commonly used when baking, as they make it much easier to thoroughly beat, whisk, knead, combine, or simply mix any kind of dough or batter. The machine normally sits or "stands" on the kitchen counter, hence the name. If you don't have one, you can use a large mixing bowl and a hand mixer.

INGREDIENTS

BUTTER
Butter generally comes in either salted or unsalted varieties. For these recipes, when we list butter, we are using salted butter unless we specifically state otherwise.

BUTTERFLY PEA FLOWER
This is a type of tea also known as "blue tea" due to its distinct purplish-blue color. It is a caffeine-free herbal tea with an earthy flavor similar to green tea. It readily available online and in some specialty and health shops.

FONDANT
Fondant is an edible icing. It looks and feels like play dough and can be molded or shaped to create very specific forms and creatures. It's an invaluable ingredient for making edible decorations (like those on our Cry of the Mandrake Cupcakes, page 70) when you need something that will really hold its shape.

MIRIN
Mirin is a sweet rice wine, similar to sake, used in Japanese cooking.

PEPITAS/PUMPKIN SEEDS
While pepitas and pumpkin seeds can be used interchangeably, pepitas are actually harvested from specific hull-less pumpkin varieties, known as Styrian or oilseed pumpkins. For our purposes, pepitas or pumpkin seeds will do, as there is no distinct difference in the flavor of the seeds themselves.

SUMAC
Made from ground berries of the sumac flower, this sour, acidic spice is most commonly used in Mediterranean and Middle Eastern cooking. It is particularly popular in dry rubs, marinades, and even dressings. Try sprinkling some over your food just before serving for extra flavor and a punch of color. If you're unable to find sumac at your local grocer, you can use lemon zest, but use less than what is called for, as the lemon zest has a more potent flavor.

WHITE TRUFFLE OIL
This aromatic oil is commonly made with a blend of olive oil and 2,4-dithiapentane, an aromatic molecule that gives truffles their distinctive smell.

ACKNOWLEDGMENTS

As a Harry Potter fan for more than twenty years, who even attended midnight release parties, the honor of being asked to write this book is a gift that I will treasure forever. To be able to help others celebrate the magical moments of their lives within the context of this magical world is magnificent, as well as a bit daunting. To attempt to do justice to such an iconic story that has been so vividly brought to life on-screen while simultaneously making recreating elements of it accessible for at-home entertaining, was not without its share of anxieties. But it is my fervent wish that the guide you hold in your hands will assist you as you gather with your loved ones and will spark ideas for you to take what you see here and make it your own.

I want to thank my daughter, Emmaleigh, for her endless ideas and encouragement as well as my mom, Lucinda, and my friends and family who supported the creative process and accepted the sacrifice of time it took to birth this book with grace. I also want to thank Hilary, Elena, Kelly, Robin, and Debra for the inspired creativity, imagination, and hard work that went into making this book even more wonderful than I had hoped.

ABOUT THE AUTHOR

Jennifer Carroll is an author, event designer, and photographer who is passionate about sharing recipes, crafts, DIY projects, and other ideas for making celebrations special and memorable. She has planned parties in Beverly Hills, Manhattan, and all over Virginia. Her work has been featured in print and online in *Martha Stewart Weddings*, *Country Living*, *Southern Living*, *Victoria*, *Country Sampler*, the *Huffington Post*, *Brides*, *The Knot*, and countless other publications. You can learn more about her and see more projects on her website: CelebratingEverydayLife.com.

INSIGHT EDITIONS

PO Box 3088
San Rafael, CA 94912
www.insighteditions.com

Find us on Facebook: www.facebook.com/InsightEditions
Follow us on Twitter: @insighteditions

Library of Congress Cataloging-in-Publication Data available.

ISBN: 978-1-68383-724-4

Publisher: Raoul Goff
VP of Licensing and Partnerships: Vanessa Lopez
VP of Creative: Chrissy Kwasnik
VP of Manufacturing: Alix Nicholaeff
Editorial Director: Vicki Jaeger
Senior Designer: Judy Wiatrek Trum
Editor: Hilary VandenBroek
Editorial Assistant: Anna Wostenberg
Senior Production Editor: Jennifer Bentham
Production Manager: Sam Taylor
Senior Production Manager, Subsidiary Rights: Lina s Palma

Additional Recipes by: Elena Craig
Additional Crafts by: Robin King and Kelly Dearth

Lead Photographer: Ted Thomas
Photographer: Amani Wade
Photographer: Josh Harding
Prop and Food Styling: Elena Craig
Assistant Prop Stylist: Wes Anderson
Assistant Food Stylist: August Craig
Assistant Prop Stylist and Balloon Wrangler Extraordinaire: Patricia Parrish

Thank you to our models: Ashleigh, Brandon, Brianna, Courtney, Devin, Jaya, Josh, Karina,
Kelsey, Luna, Lydia, Madison, Opal, Raymond, Reina, Skylaer, Violet, and Zolin.

A very special thank you to everyone at Rusty Hinges Ranch in Petaluma, California, and to
Ted Thomas for providing such a spectacular backdrop to many of the photos in this book.

ROOTS of PEACE   REPLANTED PAPER

Insight Editions, in association with Roots of Peace, will plant two trees for each tree used in the manufacturing
of this book. Roots of Peace is an internationally renowned humanitarian organization dedicated to eradicating
land mines worldwide and converting war-torn lands into productive farms and wildlife habitats. Roots of Peace
will plant two million fruit and nut trees in Afghanistan and provide farmers there with the skills and support
necessary for sustainable land use.

Manufactured in China by Insight Editions

10 9 8 7 6 5 4 3 2 1

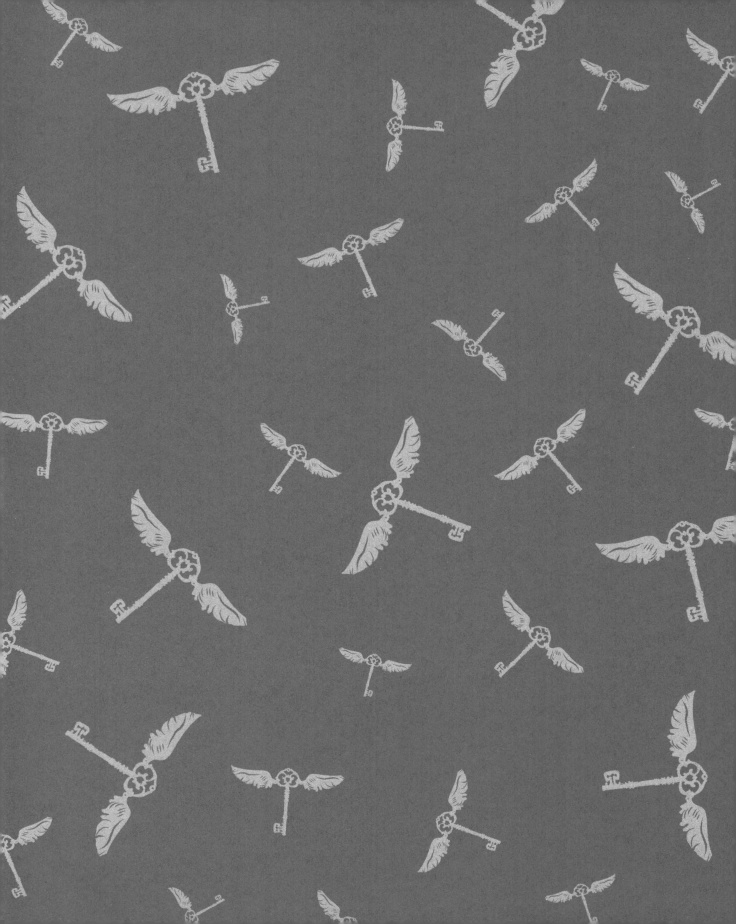

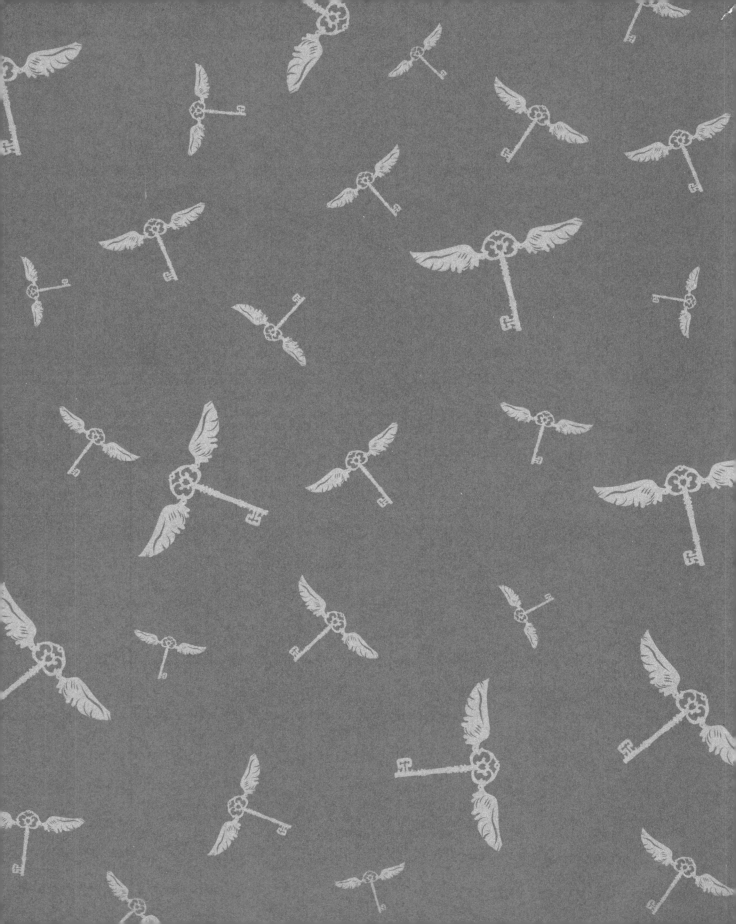